EURIP

THE BACCHAE

IPHIGENIA IN AULIS

THE CYCLOPS

RHESUS

THE COMPLETE GREEK TRAGEDIES

Edited by David Grene & Richmond Lattimore

THIRD EDITION   *Edited by Mark Griffith & Glenn W. Most*

EURIPIDES V

THE BACCHAE   *Translated by William Arrowsmith*

IPHIGENIA IN AULIS   *Translated by Charles R. Walker*

THE CYCLOPS   *Translated by William Arrowsmith*

RHESUS   *Translated by Richmond Lattimore*

The University of Chicago Press   CHICAGO & LONDON

MARK GRIFFITH is professor of classics and of theater, dance, and performance studies at the University of California, Berkeley.

GLENN W. MOST is professor of ancient Greek at the Scuola Normale Superiore at Pisa and a visiting member of the Committee on Social Thought at the University of Chicago.

DAVID GRENE (1913–2002) taught classics for many years at the University of Chicago.

RICHMOND LATTIMORE (1906–1984), professor of Greek at Bryn Mawr College, was a poet and translator best known for his translations of the Greek classics, especially his versions of the *Iliad* and the *Odyssey*.

The University of Chicago Press, Chicago 60637
The University of Chicago Press, Ltd., London
© 2013 by The University of Chicago

The Cyclops © 1952, 2013 by The University of Chicago
Rhesus, Iphigenia in Aulis © 1958, 2013 by The University of Chicago
The Bacchae © 1959, 2013 by The University of Chicago

22 21 20 19 18 17 16 15 14 13   2 3 4 5

ISBN-13: 978-0-226-30897-5 (cloth)
ISBN-13: 978-0-226-30898-2 (paper)
ISBN-13: 978-0-226-30933-0 (e-book)
ISBN-10: 0-226-30897-9 (cloth)
ISBN-10: 0-226-30898-7 (paper)
ISBN-10: 0-226-30933-9 (e-book)

Library of Congress Cataloging-in-Publication Data
Euripides.
 [Works. English. 2012]
 Euripides. — Third edition.
 volumes cm. — (The complete Greek tragedies)
 ISBN 978-0-226-30879-1 (v. 1 : cloth : alk. paper) — ISBN 0-226-30879-0 (v. 1 : cloth : alk. paper) — ISBN 978-0-226-30880-7 (v. 1 : pbk. : alk. paper) — ISBN 0-226-30880-4 (v. 1 : pbk. : alk. paper) — ISBN 978-0-226-30934-7 (v. 1 : e-book) — ISBN 0-226-30934-7 (v. 1 : e-book) — ISBN 978-0-226-30877-7 (v. 2 : cloth : alk. paper) — ISBN 0-226-30877-4 (v. 2 : cloth : alk. paper) — ISBN 978-0-226-30878-4 (v. 2 : pbk. : alk. paper) — ISBN-10: 0-226-30878-2 (v. 2 : pbk. : alk. paper) —ISBN 978-0-226-30935-4 (v. 2 : e-book) — ISBN-10: 0-226-30935-5 (v. 2 : e-book) —ISBN 978-0-226-30881-4 (v. 3 : cloth : alk. paper) — ISBN 0-226-30881-2 (v. 3 : cloth : alk. paper) — ISBN 978-0-226-30882-1 (v. 3 : pbk. : alk. paper) — ISBN 0-226-30882-0 (v. 3 : pbk. : alk. paper) — ISBN 978-0-226-30936-1 (v. 3 : e-book) — ISBN 0-226-30936-3 (v. 3 : e-book)
 1. Euripides—Translations into English. 2. Mythology, Greek—Drama. I. Lattimore, Richmond Alexander, 1906–1984. II. Taplin, Oliver. III. Griffith, Mark, Ph.D. IV. Grene, David. V. Roberts, Deborah H. VI. Arrowsmith, William, 1924–1992. VII. Jones, Frank William Oliver, 1915–. VIII. Vermeule, Emily. IX. Carson, Anne, 1950–. X. Willetts, R. F. (Ronald Frederick), 1915–1999. XI. Euripides. Alcestis. English. XII. Title. XIII. Series: Complete Greek tragedies (Unnumbered)
 PA3975.A1 2012
 882′.01—dc23

                              2012015831

⊚ This paper meets the requirements of ANSI/NISO Z39.48–1992 (Permanence of Paper)

CONTENTS

EDITORS' PREFACE TO THE THIRD EDITION

The first edition of the *Complete Greek Tragedies*, edited by David Grene and Richmond Lattimore, was published by the University of Chicago Press starting in 1953. But the origins of the series go back even further. David Grene had already published his translation of three of the tragedies with the same press in 1942, and some of the other translations that eventually formed part of the Chicago series had appeared even earlier. A second edition of the series, with new translations of several plays and other changes, was published in 1991. For well over six decades, these translations have proved to be extraordinarily popular and resilient, thanks to their combination of accuracy, poetic immediacy, and clarity of presentation. They have guided hundreds of thousands of teachers, students, and other readers toward a reliable understanding of the surviving masterpieces of the three great Athenian tragedians: Aeschylus, Sophocles, and Euripides.

But the world changes, perhaps never more rapidly than in the past half century, and whatever outlasts the day of its appearance must eventually come to terms with circumstances very different from those that prevailed at its inception. During this same period, scholarly understanding of Greek tragedy has undergone significant development, and there have been marked changes, not only in the readers to whom this series is addressed, but also in the ways in which these texts are taught and studied in universities. These changes have prompted the University of Chicago Press to perform another, more systematic revision of the translations, and we are honored to have been entrusted with this delicate and important task.

Our aim in this third edition has been to preserve and strengthen as far as possible all those features that have made the Chicago translations successful for such a long time, while at the same time revising the texts carefully and tactfully to bring them up to date and equipping them with various kinds of subsidiary help, so they may continue to serve new generations of readers.

Our revisions have addressed the following issues:

- Wherever possible, we have kept the existing translations. But we have revised them where we found this to be necessary in order to bring them closer to the ancient Greek of the original texts or to replace an English idiom that has by now become antiquated or obscure. At the same time, we have done our utmost to respect the original translator's individual style and meter.

- In a few cases, we have decided to substitute entirely new translations for the ones that were published in earlier editions of the series. Euripides' *Medea* has been newly translated by Oliver Taplin, *The Children of Heracles* by Mark Griffith, *Andromache* by Deborah Roberts, and *Iphigenia among the Taurians* by Anne Carson. We have also, in the case of Aeschylus, added translations and brief discussions of the fragments of lost plays that originally belonged to connected tetralogies along with the surviving tragedies, since awareness of these other lost plays is often crucial to the interpretation of the surviving ones. And in the case of Sophocles, we have included a translation of the substantial fragmentary remains of one of his satyr-dramas, *The Trackers* (*Ichneutai*). (See "How the Plays Were Originally Staged" below for explanation of "tetralogy," "satyr-drama," and other terms.)

- We have altered the distribution of the plays among the various volumes in order to reflect the chronological order in which they were written, when this is known or can be estimated with some probability. Thus the *Oresteia* appears now as volume 2 of Aeschylus' tragedies, and the sequence of Euripides' plays has been rearranged.

- We have rewritten the stage directions to make them more consistent throughout, keeping in mind current scholarly understanding of how Greek tragedies were staged in the fifth century BCE. In general, we have refrained from extensive stage directions of an interpretive kind, since these are necessarily speculative and modern scholars often disagree greatly about them. The Greek manuscripts themselves contain no stage directions at all.

- We have indicated certain fundamental differences in the meters and modes of delivery of all the verse of these plays. Spoken language (a kind of heightened ordinary speech, usually in the iambic trimeter rhythm) in which the characters of tragedy regularly engage in dialogue and monologue is printed in ordinary Roman font; the sung verse of choral and individual lyric odes (using a large variety of different meters), and the chanted verse recited by the chorus or individual characters (always using the anapestic meter), are rendered in *italics*, with parentheses added where necessary to indicate whether the passage is sung or chanted. In this way, readers will be able to tell at a glance how the playwright intended a given passage to be delivered in the theater, and how these shifting dynamics of poetic register contribute to the overall dramatic effect.

- All the Greek tragedies that survive alternate scenes of action or dialogue, in which individual actors speak all the lines, with formal songs performed by the chorus. Occasionally individual characters sing formal songs too, or they and the chorus may alternate lyrics and spoken verse within the same scene. Most of the formal songs are structured as a series of pairs of stanzas of which the metrical form of the first one ("strophe") is repeated exactly by a second one ("antistrophe"). Thus the metrical structure will be, e.g., strophe A, antistrophe A, strophe B, antistrophe B, with each pair of stanzas consisting of a different sequence of rhythms. Occasionally a short stanza in a different metrical form ("mesode") is inserted in the middle between one strophe and the corresponding antistrophe, and sometimes the end of the whole series is marked with a single stanza in a different metrical form ("epode")—thus, e.g., strophe A, mesode, antistrophe A; or strophe A, antistrophe A, strophe B, antistrophe B, epode. We have indicated these metrical structures by inserting the terms

STROPHE, ANTISTROPHE, MESODE, and EPODE above the first line of the relevant stanzas so that readers can easily recognize the compositional structure of these songs.

- In each play we have indicated by the symbol ° those lines or words for which there are significant uncertainties regarding the transmitted text, and we have explained as simply as possible in textual notes at the end of the volume just what the nature and degree of those uncertainties are. These notes are not at all intended to provide anything like a full scholarly apparatus of textual variants, but instead to make readers aware of places where the text transmitted by the manuscripts may not exactly reflect the poet's own words, or where the interpretation of those words is seriously in doubt.

- For each play we have provided a brief introduction that gives essential information about the first production of the tragedy, the mythical or historical background of its plot, and its reception in antiquity and thereafter.

- For each of the three great tragedians we have provided an introduction to his life and work. It is reproduced at the beginning of each volume containing his tragedies.

- We have also provided at the end of each volume a glossary explaining the names of all persons and geographical features that are mentioned in any of the plays in that volume.

It is our hope that our work will help ensure that these translations continue to delight, to move, to astonish, to disturb, and to instruct many new readers in coming generations.

MARK GRIFFITH, *Berkeley*
GLENN W. MOST, *Florence*

INTRODUCTION TO EURIPIDES

Little is known about the life of Euripides. He was probably born between 485 and 480 BCE on the island of Salamis near Athens. Of the three great writers of Athenian tragedy of the fifth century he was thus the youngest: Aeschylus was older by about forty years, Sophocles by ten or fifteen. Euripides is not reported to have ever engaged significantly in the political or military life of his city, unlike Aeschylus, who fought against the Persians at Marathon, and Sophocles, who was made a general during the Peloponnesian War. In 408 Euripides left Athens to go to the court of King Archelaus of Macedonia in Pella (we do not know exactly why). He died there in 406.

Ancient scholars knew of about ninety plays attributed to Euripides, and he was given permission to participate in the annual tragedy competition at the festival of Dionysus on twenty-two occasions—strong evidence of popular interest in his work. But he was not particularly successful at winning the first prize. Although he began competing in 455 (the year after Aeschylus died), he did not win first place until 441, and during his lifetime he received that award only four times; a fifth victory was bestowed on him posthumously for his trilogy *Iphigenia in Aulis*, *Bacchae*, *Alcmaeon in Corinth* (this last play is lost), produced by one of his sons who was also named Euripides. By contrast, Aeschylus won thirteen victories and Sophocles eighteen. From various references, especially the frequent parodies of Euripides in the comedies of Aristophanes, we can surmise that many members of contemporary Athenian audiences objected to Euripides' tendency to make the characters of tragedy more modern and less heroic, to represent the passions of women, and to reflect recent developments in philosophy and music.

But in the centuries after his death, Euripides went on to become by far the most popular of the Greek tragedians. When the ancient Greeks use the phrase "the poet" without further specification and do not mean by it Homer, they always mean Euripides. Hundreds of fragments from his plays, mostly quite short, are found in quotations by other authors and in anthologies from the period between the third century BCE and the fourth century CE. Many more fragments of his plays have been preserved on papyrus starting in the fourth century BCE than of those by Aeschylus and Sophocles together, and far more scenes of his plays have been associated with images on ancient pottery starting in the same century and on frescoes in Pompeii and elsewhere and Roman sarcophagi some centuries later than is the case for either of his rivals. Some knowledge of his texts spread far and wide through collections of sententious aphorisms and excerpts of speeches and songs drawn from his plays (or invented in his name).

It was above all in the schools that Euripides became the most important author of tragedies: children throughout the Greek-speaking world learned the rules of language and comportment by studying first and foremost Homer and Euripides. But we know that Euripides' plays also continued to be performed in theaters for centuries, and the transmitted texts of some of the more popular ones (e.g., *Medea*, *Orestes*) seem to bear the traces of modifications by ancient producers and actors. Both in his specific plays and plots and in his general conception of dramatic action and character, Euripides massively influenced later Greek playwrights, not only tragic poets but also comic ones (especially Menander, the most important dramatist of New Comedy, born about a century and a half after Euripides)—and not only Greek ones, but Latin ones as well, such as Accius and Pacuvius, and later Seneca (who went on to exert a deep influence on Renaissance drama).

A more or less complete collection of his plays was made in

Alexandria during the third century BCE. Whereas, out of all the plays of Aeschylus and Sophocles, only seven tragedies each were chosen (no one knows by whom) at some point later in antiquity, probably in the second century CE, to represent their work, Euripides received the distinction of having ten plays selected as canonical: *Alcestis, Andromache, Bacchae, Hecuba, Hippolytus, Medea, Orestes, The Phoenician Women, Rhesus* (scholars generally think this play was written by someone other than Euripides and was attributed to him in antiquity by mistake), and *The Trojan Women*. Of these ten tragedies, three—*Hecuba, Orestes*, and *The Phoenician Women*—were especially popular in the Middle Ages; they are referred to as the Byzantine triad, after the capital of the eastern Empire, Byzantium, known later as Constantinople and today as Istanbul.

The plays that did not form part of the selection gradually ceased to be copied, and thus most of them eventually were lost to posterity. We would possess only these ten plays and fragments of the others were it not for the lucky chance that a single volume of an ancient complete edition of Euripides' plays, arranged alphabetically, managed to survive into the Middle Ages. Thus we also have another nine tragedies (referred to as the alphabetic plays) whose titles in Greek all begin with the letters *epsilon, êta, iota*, and *kappa*: *Electra, Helen, The Children of Heracles (Hêrakleidai), Heracles, The Suppliants (Hiketides), Ion, Iphigenia in Aulis, Iphigenia among the Taurians*, and *The Cyclops (Kyklôps)*. The Byzantine triad have very full ancient commentaries (scholia) and are transmitted by hundreds of medieval manuscripts; the other seven plays of the canonical selection have much sparser scholia and are transmitted by something more than a dozen manuscripts; the alphabetic plays have no scholia at all and are transmitted only by a single manuscript in rather poor condition and by its copies.

Modern scholars have been able to establish a fairly secure dating for most of Euripides' tragedies thanks to the exact indications provided by ancient scholarship for the first production of some of them and the relative chronology suggested by metrical and other features for the others. Accordingly the five volumes of this third edition have been organized according to the probable chronological sequence:

Volume 1:   *Alcestis:* 438 BCE
            Medea: 431
            The Children of Heracles: ca. 430
            Hippolytus: 428
Volume 2:   *Andromache:* ca. 425
            Hecuba: ca. 424
            The Suppliant Women: ca. 423
            Electra: ca. 420
Volume 3:   *Heracles:* ca. 415
            The Trojan Women: 415
            Iphigenia among the Taurians: ca. 414
            Ion: ca. 413
Volume 4:   *Helen:* 412
            The Phoenician Women: ca. 409
            Orestes: 408
Volume 5:   *Bacchae:* posthumously after 406
            Iphigenia in Aulis: posthumously after 406
            The Cyclops: date unknown
            Rhesus: probably spurious, from the fourth
            century BCE

In the Renaissance Euripides remained the most popular of the three tragedians. Directly and by the mediation of Seneca he influenced drama from the sixteenth to the eighteenth century far more than Aeschylus or Sophocles did. But toward the end of the eighteenth century and even more in the course of the nineteenth century, he came increasingly under attack yet again, as already in the fifth century BCE, and for much the same reason, as being decadent, tawdry, irreligious, and inharmonious. He was also criticized for his perceived departures from the ideal of "the tragic" (as exemplified by plays such as Sophocles' *Oedipus the King* and *Antigone*), especially in the "romance" plots of *Alcestis,*

Iphigenia among the Taurians, Ion, and *Helen.* It was left to the twentieth century to discover its own somewhat disturbing affinity to his tragic style and worldview. Nowadays among theatrical audiences, scholars, and nonprofessional readers Euripides is once again at least as popular as his two rivals.

HOW THE PLAYS WERE ORIGINALLY STAGED

Nearly all the plays composed by Aeschylus, Sophocles, and Euripides were first performed in the Theater of Dionysus at Athens, as part of the annual festival and competition in drama. This was not only a literary and musical event, but also an important religious and political ceremony for the Athenian community. Each year three tragedians were selected to compete, with each of them presenting four plays per day, a "tetralogy" of three tragedies and one satyr-play. The satyr-play was a type of drama similar to tragedy in being based on heroic myth and employing many of the same stylistic features, but distinguished by having a chorus of half-human, half-horse followers of Dionysus—sileni or satyrs—and by always ending happily. Extant examples of this genre are Euripides' *The Cyclops* (in *Euripides*, vol. 5) and Sophocles' *The Trackers* (partially preserved: in *Sophocles*, vol. 2).

The three competing tragedians were ranked by a panel of citizens functioning as amateur judges, and the winner received an honorific prize. Records of these competitions were maintained, allowing Aristotle and others later to compile lists of the dates when each of Aeschylus', Sophocles', and Euripides' plays were first performed and whether they placed first, second, or third in the competition (unfortunately we no longer possess the complete lists).

The tragedians competed on equal terms: each had at his disposal three actors (only two in Aeschylus' and Euripides' earliest plays) who would often have to switch between roles as each play progressed, plus other nonspeaking actors to play attendants and other subsidiary characters; a chorus of twelve (in Aeschylus' time) or fifteen (for most of the careers of Sophocles and Euripides), who would sing and dance formal songs and whose Chorus Leader would engage in dialogue with the characters or offer comment on the action; and a pipe-player, to accompany the sung portions of the play.

All the performers were men, and the actors and chorus members all wore masks. The association of masks with other Dionysian rituals may have affected their use in the theater; but masks had certain practical advantages as well—for example, making it easy to play female characters and to change quickly between roles. In general, the use of masks also meant that ancient acting techniques must have been rather different from what we are used to seeing in the modern theater. Acting in a mask requires a more frontal and presentational style of performance toward the audience than is usual with unmasked, "realistic" acting; a masked actor must communicate far more by voice and stylized bodily gesture than by facial expression, and the gradual development of a character in the course of a play could hardly be indicated by changes in his or her mask. Unfortunately, however, we know almost nothing about the acting techniques of the Athenian theater. But we do know that the chorus members were all Athenian amateurs, and so were the actors up until the later part of the fifth century, by which point a prize for the best actor had been instituted in the tragic competition, and the art of acting (which of course included solo singing and dancing) was becoming increasingly professionalized.

The tragedian himself not only wrote the words for his play but also composed the music and choreography and directed the productions. It was said that Aeschylus also acted in his plays but that Sophocles chose not to, except early in his career, because his voice was too weak. Euripides is reported to have had a collaborator who specialized in musical composition. The costs for each playwright's production were shared between an individual wealthy citizen, as a kind of "super-tax" requirement, and the city.

The Theater of Dionysus itself during most of the fifth century BCE probably consisted of a large rectangular or trapezoidal dance floor, backed by a one-story wooden building (the *skênê*), with a large central door that opened onto the dance floor. (Some scholars have argued that two doors were used, but the evidence is thin.) Between the *skênê* and the dance floor there may have been a narrow stage on which the characters acted and which communicated easily with the dance floor. For any particular play, the *skênê* might represent a palace, a house, a temple, or a cave, for example; the interior of this "building" was generally invisible to the audience, with all the action staged in front of it. Sophocles is said to have been the first to use painted scenery; this must have been fairly simple and easy to remove, as every play had a different setting. Playwrights did not include stage directions in their texts. Instead, a play's setting was indicated explicitly by the speaking characters.

All the plays were performed in the open air and in daylight. Spectators sat on wooden seats in rows, probably arranged in rectangular blocks along the curving slope of the Acropolis. (The stone semicircular remains of the Theater of Dionysus that are visible today in Athens belong to a later era.) Seating capacity seems to have been four to six thousand—thus a mass audience, but not quite on the scale of the theaters that came to be built during the fourth century BCE and later at Epidaurus, Ephesus, and many other locations all over the Mediterranean.

Alongside the *skênê*, on each side, there were passages through which actors could enter and exit. The acting area included the dance floor, the doorway, and the area immediately in front of the *skênê*. Occasionally an actor appeared on the roof or above it, as if flying. He was actually hanging from a crane (*mêchanê*: hence *deus ex machina*, "a god from the machine"). The *skênê* was also occasionally opened up—the mechanical details are uncertain—in order to show the audience what was concealed within (usually dead bodies). Announcements of entrances and exits, like the setting, were made by the characters. Although the medieval manuscripts of the surviving plays do not provide explicit stage directions, it is usually possible to infer from the words or from the context whether a particular entrance or exit is being made through a door (into the *skênê*) or by one of the side entrances. In later antiquity, there may have been a rule that one side entrance always led to the city center, the other to the countryside or harbor. Whether such a rule was ever observed in the fifth century is uncertain.

THE BACCHAE

Translated by WILLIAM ARROWSMITH

THE BACCHAE: INTRODUCTION

The Play: Date and Composition

Euripides' *Bacchae* was first produced posthumously at the Great Dionysian festival in 405 BCE. Euripides had left Athens for Macedonia three years earlier and had died there in 406. The *Bacchae* was staged in his absence by one of his sons (also named Euripides), together with *Iphigenia in Aulis* (preserved) and *Alcmaeon in Corinth* (lost); this tetralogy won first prize for Euripides after his death, an award that he had won only four times during his lifetime.

The Myth

Euripides' *Bacchae* is the only surviving Greek tragedy to focus on a myth concerning Dionysus himself (otherwise known as Bacchus, or Bromius), the god of wine and theater in whose honor all these tragedies were performed. This play dramatizes Dionysus' establishment of his first cult in Greece, in the city of Thebes; it quickly became the classic version of the story. Dionysus had been conceived in Thebes as the son of Zeus by Cadmus' daughter, the mortal woman Semele, but she had been blasted by the god's thunderbolt before she could give birth to the child. The unborn infant Dionysus was rescued by Zeus, and in due course was born from Zeus' thigh; then after growing up he proceeded triumphantly throughout much of Asia, introducing his rites among the various peoples there. Now, accompanied by Asian bacchants, he has returned to Thebes, where the original ruler, Cadmus, has abdicated in favor of his grandson Pentheus. Semele's sisters, including Pentheus' mother, Agave, are denying her claim that Dionysus was the fruit of her union with a god, and Dionysus has punished them by driving all the women of Thebes mad and sending them in a frenzy out from the city onto the nearby mountain Cithaeron.

It is at this point that the action of the play begins. Dionysus, disguised as a mortal priest of his cult, sets the scene and introduces the action; only the audience knows his true identity. First the Asian bacchants (the chorus) arrive, and then Cadmus and Teiresias, all of them dedicated in different ways to celebrating this new god's worship. Pentheus rushes in, agitated at the news of the foreigner's arrival, and proceeds to do all he can to suppress the new cult and its representatives, even attempting to lock up the stranger (the disguised Dionysus) in prison and to capture the Theban bacchants on the mountainside. His efforts fail humiliatingly, yet he still cannot recognize the reality of Dionysus' power, despite being fascinated with the women's activities on Cithaeron. Eventually, at Dionysus' suggestion, Pentheus agrees to disguise himself as a bacchant himself and to go spy upon them. There he ends up being torn to pieces by Agave and the others, who in their crazed state mistake him for a lion. As the play comes to a close, Agave comes to realize what she has done. She and her father, Cadmus, go into exile, in misery, and Dionysus proclaims his future worship throughout Greece.

As early as Homer's *Iliad*, various myths told of the establishment of cults of Dionysus despite bitter human resistance, and of the god's bloody vengeance upon such unbelievers as Pentheus and the Thracian king Lycurgus. Scholars disagree about whether, and if so to what extent, the very earliest Athenian tragedies represented legends involving Dionysus himself. But it is certain that such myths had sometimes been presented in tragedies, now lost, by a number of playwrights before Euripides. Aeschylus composed two tetralogies on Dionysiac themes, a *Lycurgeia* (comprising *Edonians*, *Bassarai* [a term for Thracian bacchants], *Youths*, and the satyr-play *Lycurgus*) and a Theban tetralogy (including probably *Semele*, *Wool-Carders*, *Pentheus*, and the satyr-play *Nurses*). Lesser known tragedians wrote other plays on the subject: Polyphrasmon a tetralogy on Lycurgus, Xenocles a *Bacchae*, Sophocles' son Iophon a *Bacchae* or *Pentheus*, Spintharos a *Lightning-Struck Semele*, Cleophon a *Bacchae*; and, probably later than Euripides, Chaeremon wrote a *Dionysus*, Carcinus a *Semele*, and Diogenes too a *Semele*. Little or nothing is known about most of these plays, but when fragments or reports have survived, they usually indicate striking affinities with Euripides' play. In particular, the fragments of Aeschylus' *Lycurgeia* show an effeminate Dionysus being captured and interrogated, the bacchants being imprisoned and miraculously escaping, and the house shaking in a bacchic frenzy. So at least in its general outline and in some of its incidents Euripides' play will not have seemed entirely unusual to its first audience, though some scenes—perhaps especially Teiresias' sophistic lecture on Dionysian religion and the whole gruesome episode of Agave—are likely to have been surprising Euripidean innovations.

What is Euripides' own attitude to the story and characters he has dramatized in *The Bacchae*? Is this play his final declaration of faith in traditional Greek religion, a recantation of the notorious expressions of doubt made by some of the characters in his earlier plays? Or is it a denunciation of the catastrophes to which religious fanaticism can lead? To what extent may we imagine that elements of actual Dionysian ritual are being represented in the scenes of dance, cross-dressing, and collective dismemberment of a victim? Certainly the benefits that Dionysus provides—wine, music, and dance, as well as temporary release from toil and worry, especially for women, laborers, and the socially marginalized—are vividly and eloquently presented, both by the chorus and by several characters in the play. At the same time, the violence and wild behavior of some of the god's crazed worshippers are shocking and disturbing. In the end, the play leaves the audience in no doubt as to the disastrous consequences of rejecting Dionysus, even as it also reminds us of the ambiguous delights— and dangers—of the altered states, disguises, and transgressions of norms that his worship traditionally brings and that theater especially thrives on. To what extent does the play explore the crucial but ambiguous relation of Dionysian drama to politics and the dangers to which a city exposes itself if it refuses to accept tragedy within its walls? In any case, Euripides' decision, in self-imposed exile at the Macedonian court (where tragedy appears by this date to have become almost as popular as in Athens), to compose this play—perhaps his last completed one—for production at the Great Dionysian festival back home in Athens raises questions that have always fascinated not only scholars but also ordinary readers and theatergoers.

Transmission and Reception

The evidence of quotations and allusions among later authors and the survival of at least eight papyri containing fragments of the play indicate that *The Bacchae* was quite popular throughout antiquity. The tragedy is frequently referred to by pagan and Christian writers, and it deeply influenced a number of later works of Greek literature, especially the *Dionysiaca*, a forty-eight-book epic on Dionysus (the longest surviving poem from antiquity) by the early fifth-century CE poet Nonnus, and *The Passion of Christ*, an anonymous Byzantine Christian cento (a poem made up entirely of recycled verses from earlier poetry) which uses many lines from Euripides' tragedy about the experiences of Dionysus (as well as verses from other plays, especially by Aeschylus and Euripides) to tell of Jesus' sufferings and resurrection. So too, in Latin literature Euripides' play seems to have been a model for the Roman tragedians Pacuvius for his *Pentheus* and Accius for his *Bacchae* (whereas Naevius seems in his *Lycurgus* to have gone back to Aeschylus); but unfortunately none of these plays survive.

Directly and indirectly, Euripides' *Bacchae* remained a vital presence not only in ancient schoolrooms but also on ancient stages—one bizarre but striking piece of evidence is an incident at the Parthian court in 53 BCE when an actor dressed as Agave sang her lines *"We bring this branch to the palace, / this fresh-cut tendril from the mountains. / Happy was the hunting"* (1169-71) to general applause while holding the severed head of the defeated

Roman general Crassus. And somewhat over a century later the emperor Nero may have sung excerpts from the play while accompanying himself on the kithara. But scholars disagree about whether this tragedy left substantial traces in ancient pictorial art: a number of vases and frescoes depict the death of Pentheus, and scenes of Dionysiac revelry are frequent in all forms of ancient art, including sarcophagi, but it is unclear to what extent these are related directly to Euripides' play.

The Bacchae seems to have been selected as one of the ten canonical plays most studied and read in antiquity, but it was probably the very last play in that edition and as a result was more liable to damage, particularly at its ending. In fact, it is transmitted to us only by one manuscript and its copy; the former breaks off about halfway through, at line 755, so for the rest of the play we are dependent upon a single manuscript—and that one has at least one large gap near the end and a couple of smaller ones. Editors use a combination of different sources—summaries, citations, and allusions from other authors, verses from *The Passion of Christ*, and papyri—to try to fill out that large gap, at least speculatively. Unlike the other plays in the collection of ten, *The Bacchae* does not have any ancient or medieval commentaries.

In modern times, it was not until the end of the eighteenth century that *The Bacchae* began to be regarded as one of the supreme achievements of Greek tragedy, and also as crucial evidence for the religious significance of Dionysus in antiquity. This development began in Germany, with the poets Friedrich Hölderlin (who began, but did not complete, a translation of the play in 1799 and composed a number of poems about Dionysus and Jesus) and Johann Wolfgang von Goethe (who translated the whole play starting in 1821); and it culminated there in the philosopher Friedrich Nietzsche, whose *Birth of Tragedy* (1872) conceived of the Dionysian element as a vital counter to the Apollinian one in ancient Greek and also in contemporary European culture. Thereafter, it is difficult to separate the influence of Euripides from that of Nietzsche, among such authors as Hugo von Hofmannsthal ("Pentheus," 1904: a dramatic sketch), Robinson Jeffers ("The

Women on Cythaeron," 1928, a poem, later retitled "The Humanist's Tragedy"), Egon Wellesz (*The Bacchants*, 1931, an opera), Martha Graham (*Three Choric Dances for an Antique Greek Tragedy*, 1933), W. H. Auden (with Chester Kallman, the libretto for Hans Werner Henze's opera *The Bassarids*, 1966), and Donna Tartt (*The Secret History*, 1992, a novel). Starting in the late 1960s, the play was staged ever more frequently as a celebration of erotic, musical, and hippy vitality, a questioning of traditional masculinity and gender roles, and a condemnation of prudish censoriousness: the production by Richard Schechner and the Living Theater, *Dionysus in '69*, was a controversial milestone. Other recent notable dramatic versions include Joe Orton's *The Erpingham Camp* (1966), Nigerian author Wole Soyinka's *The Bacchae of Euripides: A Communion Rite* (first staged 1973), and Brad Mays' staging at the Complex in Los Angeles (1997, filmed 2000). Euripides' *Bacchae* continues to be one of the most frequently produced and read of all Greek tragedies, one of the most popular—and one of the most perplexing.

THE BACCHAE

Characters DIONYSUS (also called Bacchus, Bromius,
Dithyrambus, Euhius, and Iacchus)
CHORUS of Asian Bacchae (female followers of
Dionysus, also called Bacchants and maenads)
TEIRESIAS, Theban seer
CADMUS, father of Semele (Dionysus' mother)
and of Agave
PENTHEUS, king of Thebes
ATTENDANT of Pentheus
FIRST MESSENGER, a shepherd
SECOND MESSENGER, a servant of Pentheus
AGAVE, daughter of Cadmus, mother of
Pentheus

*Scene: Pentheus' palace at Thebes. In front of it stands the tomb of
Semele.*

(Enter Dionysus from the side.)

DIONYSUS
    I am Dionysus, the son of Zeus,
come back to Thebes, this land where I was born.
My mother was Cadmus' daughter, Semele by name,
midwived by fire, delivered by the lightning's
blast.
    And here I stand, a god incognito,
disguised as man, beside the stream of Dirce   5
and the waters of Ismenus. There before the palace

I see my lightning-blasted mother's grave,
and there upon the ruins of her shattered house
the living fire of Zeus still smolders on
in deathless witness of Hera's violence and rage
against my mother. But Cadmus wins my praise: 10
he has made this tomb a shrine, sacred to his daughter.
It was I who screened her grave with the green
of the clustering vine.

                    Far behind me lie
the gold-rich lands of Lydia and Phrygia,
where my journeying began. Overland I went,
across the steppes of Persia where the sun strikes hotly
down, through Bactrian fastness and the grim waste   15
of Media. Thence to blessed Arabia I came;
and so, along all Asia's swarming littoral
of towered cities where barbarians and Greeks,
mingling, live, my progress made. There
I taught my dances to the feet of living men,
establishing my mysteries and rites
that I might be revealed to mortals for what I am:
a god.

        And thence to Thebes.

                    This city, first   20
in Hellas, now shrills and echoes to my women's cries,
their ecstasy of joy. Here in Thebes
I bound the fawnskin to the women's flesh and armed
their hands with shafts of ivy. For I have come   25
to refute that slander spoken by my mother's sisters—
those who least had right to slander her.
They said that Dionysus was no son of Zeus,
but Semele had slept beside a man in love
and foisted off her shame on Zeus—a fraud, they sneered,   30
contrived by Cadmus to protect his daughter's name.
They said she lied, and Zeus in anger at that lie
blasted her with lightning.

                    Because of that offense
I have stung them with frenzy, hounded them from home
up to the mountains where they wander, crazed of mind,
and compelled them to wear my ritual uniform.
Every woman in Thebes—but the women only—   35
I drove from home, mad. There they sit,
all of them, together with the daughters of Cadmus,
beneath the silver firs on the roofless rocks.
Like it or not, this city must learn its lesson:
it lacks initiation in my mysteries;   40
so I shall vindicate my mother Semele
and stand revealed to mortal eyes as the god
she bore to Zeus.
                    Cadmus the king has abdicated,
leaving his throne and power to his grandson Pentheus,
who revolts against divinity, in me;   45
thrusts me from his offerings; omits my name
from his prayers. Therefore I shall prove to him
and everyone in Thebes that I am god
indeed. And when my worship is established here,
and all is well, then I shall go my way
and be revealed to other men in other lands.   50
But if the town of Thebes attempts to force
my Bacchae from the mountainside with weapons,
I shall marshal my maenads and take the field.
To these ends I have laid divinity aside
and go disguised as man.

                              (*Calling toward the side.*)

                    On, my women,   55
women who worship me, women whom I led
out of Asia where Tmolus heaves its rampart
over Lydia!
                    On, comrades of my progress here!
Come, and with your native Phrygian drum—

Rhea's invention and mine—pound at the doors   60
of Pentheus' palace! Let the city of Thebes behold you,
while I myself go to Cithaeron's glens
where my Bacchae wait, and join their whirling dances.

(*Exit Dionysus to one side. Enter the Chorus
of Asian Bacchae from the other.*)

CHORUS [*singing*]
   Out of the land of Asia,
   down from holy Tmolus,   65
   speeding the god's service,
   for Bromius we come!
   Hard are the labors of god;
   hard, but his service is sweet.
   Sweet to serve, sweet to cry:
                        Bacchus! Euhoi!
   You on the streets! You on the roads!
   You in the palace! Come out!
   Let every mouth be hushed.   70
   Let no ill-omened words
   profane your tongues.
   For now I shall raise the old, old hymn to Dionysus.

                    STROPHE A
   Blessed, those who know the god's mysteries,°
   happy those who sanctify their lives,
   whose souls are initiated into the holy company,   75
   dancing on the mountains the holy dance of the god,
   and those who keep the rites of Cybele the Mother,
   and who shake the thyrsus,   80
   who wear the crown of ivy.
   Dionysus is their god!
   On, Bacchae, on, you Bacchae,
   bring the god, son of god,
   bring Bromius home,   85
   from Phrygian mountains,
   to the broad streets of Hellas—Bromius!

His mother bore him once in labor bitter;
lightning-struck, forced by fire that flared from Zeus,   90
consumed, she died, untimely torn,
in childbed dead by blow of light!
Zeus it was who saved his son,   95
swiftly bore him to a private place,
concealed his son from Hera's eyes
in his thigh as in a womb,
binding it with clasps of gold.
And when the weaving Fates fulfilled the time,   100
the bull-horned god was born of Zeus.
He crowned his son with garlands,
wherefrom descends to us the maenad's writhing crown,
wild creatures in our hair.

STROPHE B

O Thebes, nurse of Semele,   105
   crown your head with ivy!
   Grow green with bryony!
   Redden with berries! O city,
   with boughs of oak and fir,   110
   come dance the dance of god!
   Fringe your skins of dappled fawn
   with tufts of twisted wool!
   Handle with holy care
   the violent wand of god!
And at once the whole land shall dance
when Bromius leads the holy company   115
to the mountain!

                to the mountain!
where the throng of women waits,
driven from shuttle and loom,
possessed by Dionysus!

ANTISTROPHE B

And I praise the holies of Crete,   120

the caves of the dancing Curetes,
there where Zeus was born,
where helmed in triple tier
the Corybantes invented this leather drum. 125
They were the first of all
whose whirling feet kept time
to the strict beat of the taut hide
and the sweet cry of the Phrygian pipes.
Then from them to Rhea's hands
the holy drum was handed down,
to give the beat for maenads' dances;
and, taken up by the raving satyrs, 130
it now accompanies the dance
which every other year
celebrates your name:
     Dionysus!

EPODE

He is sweet upon the mountains, when he drops to the earth 135
     from the running packs.
   He wears the holy fawnskin. He hunts the wild goat
     and kills it.
   He delights in raw flesh.
   He runs to the mountains of Phrygia, of Lydia, 140
   Bromius, who leads us! Euhoi!
     With milk the earth flows! It flows with wine!
   It runs with the nectar of bees!
     Like frankincense in its fragrance
is the blaze of the torch he bears, 145
   flaming from his trailing fennel wand
     as he runs, as he dances,
   kindling the stragglers,
     spurring with cries,
   and his long curls stream to the wind! 150
And he cries, as they cry,°
     "On, Bacchae!

> *On, Bacchae!*
> *Follow, glory of golden Tmolus,*
> *hymning Dionysus*   155
> *with a rumble of drums,*
> *with the cry, Euhoi! to the Euhoian god,*
> *with cries in Phrygian melodies,*
> *when the holy pipe like honey plays*   160
> *the sacred song for those who go*
> *to the mountain!*
>   *to the mountain!"*   165
> *Then, in ecstasy, like a colt by its grazing mother,*
> *the bacchant runs with flying feet, she leaps!*

*(Enter Teiresias from the side, dressed in the bacchant's
fawnskin and ivy crown, and carrying a thyrsus.)*

TEIRESIAS

Ho there, who keeps the gates?
                  Summon Cadmus—   170
Cadmus, Agenor's son, who came from Sidon
and built the towers of our Thebes.
              Go, someone.
Say Teiresias wants him. He will know what errand
brings me, that agreement, age with age, we made   175
to deck our wands, to dress in skins of fawn
and crown our heads with ivy.

(Enter Cadmus from the palace, dressed like Teiresias.)

CADMUS

           My old friend,
I knew it must be you when I heard your summons.
For there's a wisdom in his voice that makes
the man of wisdom known.
            So here I am,
dressed in the costume of the god, prepared to go.   180
Insofar as we are able, Teiresias, we must
do honor to this god, for he was born

my daughter's son, who has been revealed to men,°
the god, Dionysus.

          Where shall we go, where
shall we tread the dance, tossing our white-haired heads
in the dances of the god?

          Expound to me, Teiresias,   185
age to age: for you are wise.

                   Surely
I could dance night and day, untiringly
beating the earth with my thyrsus! And how sweet it is
to forget my old age.

TEIRESIAS

          It is the same with me.
I too feel young, young enough to dance.   190

CADMUS

Good. Shall we not take our chariots to the mountain?

TEIRESIAS

Walking would be better. It shows more honor
to the god.

CADMUS

          So be it. I shall lead, my old age
conducting yours.

TEIRESIAS

          The god will guide us there
with no effort on our part.

CADMUS

          Are we the only men   195
who will dance for Bacchus?

TEIRESIAS

          The others are all blind.
Only we can see.

CADMUS

But we delay too long.
Here, take my arm.

TEIRESIAS

Link my hand in yours.

CADMUS

I am a man, nothing more. I do not scoff
at gods.

TEIRESIAS

We do not trifle with divinity.°   200
No, we are the heirs of customs and traditions
hallowed by age and handed down to us
by our fathers. No quibbling logic can topple them,
whatever subtleties this clever age invents.
People may say: "Aren't you ashamed? At your age,
going dancing, wreathing your head with ivy?"   205
Well, I am not ashamed. Did the god declare
that just the young or just the old should dance?
No, he desires his honor from all mankind.
He wants no one excluded from his worship.

CADMUS

Because you cannot see, Teiresias, let me be   210
interpreter for you this time. Here comes
the man to whom I left my throne, Echion's son,
Pentheus, hastening toward the palace. He seems
excited and disturbed. What is his news?

(Enter Pentheus from the side.)

PENTHEUS

I happened to be away, out of this land,   215
but I've heard of some strange mischief in the town,
stories of our women leaving home to frisk
in mock ecstasies among the thickets on the mountain,

dancing in honor of the latest divinity,
a certain Dionysus, whoever he may be! 220
In their midst stand bowls brimming with wine.
And then, one by one, the women wander off
to hidden nooks where they serve the lusts of men.
Priestesses of Bacchus they claim they are,
but it's really Aphrodite they adore. 225
I have captured some of them; my jailers
have bound their hands and locked them in our prison.
Those who run at large shall be hunted down
out of the mountains like the animals they are—
yes, my own mother Agave, and Ino
and Autonoë, the mother of Actaeon. 230
In no time at all I shall have them trapped
in iron nets and stop this obscene disorder.

    I am also told a foreigner has come to Thebes
from Lydia, one of those charlatan magicians,
with long yellow curls smelling of perfumes, 235
with flushed cheeks and the spells of Aphrodite
in his eyes. His days and nights he spends
with women and girls, dangling before them the joys
of initiation in his mysteries.
But let me catch him in this land of mine
and I'll stop his pounding with his wand and tossing 240
his head. I'll have his head cut off his body!
And *this* is the man who claims that Dionysus
is a god and was sewn into the thigh of Zeus,
when, in point of fact, that same blast of lightning
consumed him and his mother both, for her lie 245
that she had lain with Zeus in love. Whoever
this stranger is, aren't such impostures,
such unruliness, worthy of hanging?

(He catches sight of Teiresias and Cadmus.)

             What!
But this is incredible! Teiresias the seer

tricked out in a dappled fawnskin!
And you,
you, my grandfather, playing the bacchant—what a laugh!—   250
with a fennel wand!
Sir, I shrink to see your old age
so foolish. Shake that ivy off, grandfather!
Now drop that wand. Drop it, I say.
Aha,
I see: this is your doing, Teiresias.   255
Yes, you want still another god revealed to men
so you can pocket the profits from burnt offerings
and bird-watching. By heaven, only your age
restrains me now from sending you to prison
with those Bacchic women for importing here to Thebes
these filthy mysteries. When once you see   260
the glint of wine shining at the feasts of women,
then you may be sure the festival is rotten.

CHORUS LEADER
What blasphemy! Stranger, have you no respect
for the gods? For Cadmus who sowed the dragon teeth?
Will the son of Echion disgrace his house?   265

TEIRESIAS
Give a wise man an honest brief to plead
and his eloquence is no remarkable achievement.
But you are glib; your phrases come rolling out
smoothly on the tongue, as though your words were wise
instead of foolish. The man whose glibness flows
from his conceit of speech declares the thing he is: 270
a worthless and a stupid citizen.
I tell you,
this god whom you ridicule shall someday have
enormous power and prestige throughout Hellas.
Mankind, young man, possesses two supreme blessings.
First of these is the goddess Demeter, or Earth—   275
whichever name you choose to call her by.

It was she who gave to man his nourishment of dry food.
But after her there came the son of Semele,
who matched her present by inventing liquid wine
from grapes as his gift to man. For filled with juice from
      vines,
suffering mankind forgets its grief; from it   280
comes sleep; with it oblivion of the troubles
of the day. There is no other medicine
for misery. And when we pour libations
to the gods, we pour the god of wine himself
that through his intercession man may win   285
the good things of life.
                    You sneer, do you, at that story
that Dionysus was sewn into the thigh of Zeus?
Let me teach you what that really means. When Zeus
rescued from the thunderbolt his infant son,
he brought him to Olympus. Hera, however,
plotted at heart to hurl the child from heaven.   290
Like the god he is, Zeus countered her. Breaking off
a tiny fragment of that ether which surrounds the earth,
he molded from it a substitute Dionysus.
This piece of "sky" he gave to Hera as a hostage,
and thereby saved Dionysus from Hera's hate. With time,
men garbled the word and said that he'd been sewn   295
into the "thigh" of Zeus. This was their story,
whereas, in fact, Zeus made a fake for Hera
and gave it as a hostage for his son.
                              Moreover,
this is a god of prophecy. His worshippers,
like maniacs, are endowed with mantic powers.
For when the god goes greatly into a man,   300
he drives him mad and makes him tell the future.
                    Besides,
he has usurped even some functions of warlike Ares.
Thus, at times, you see an army mustered under arms
stricken with panic before it lifts a spear.

This panic comes from Dionysus.

                              Someday   305
you shall even see him bounding with his torches
among the crags at Delphi, leaping the pastures
that stretch between the peaks, whirling and waving
his thyrsus: great throughout Hellas.

                              Mark my words,
Pentheus. Don't be so sure that domination   310
is what matters in the life of man; do not mistake
for wisdom the fantasies of a sick mind.
Welcome the god to Thebes; crown your head;
pour him libations and join his revels.

        Dionysus does not, I admit, compel a woman
to be chaste.° Always and in every case   315
it is her character and nature that keep°
a woman chaste. But even in the rites of Dionysus,
the chaste woman will not be corrupted.

                              Think:
you are pleased when men stand outside your doors
and the city glorifies the name of Pentheus.   320
And so the god: he too delights in honor.
So Cadmus, whom you ridicule, and I will crown
our heads with ivy and join the dances of the god—
an ancient gray-haired pair perhaps, but dance
we must. Nothing you have said would make me
change my mind or fight against a god.   325
You are mad, grievously mad, beyond the power
of any drugs to cure, for you are drugged
with madness.

CHORUS LEADER

                      Apollo would approve your words.
Wisely you honor Bromius: a great god.

CADMUS

                      My boy,
Teiresias advises well. Your home is here   330

with us, with our customs and traditions, not
outside, alone. You flit about, and though
you may be smart, your smartness is all nothing.
Even if this Dionysus is no god,
as you assert, persuade yourself that he is.
The falsehood is a noble one, for Semele will seem   335
to be the mother of a god, and this confers
no small distinction on our family.
                                                You see
that dreadful death your cousin Actaeon died
when those man-eating hounds he had raised himself
savaged him and tore his body limb from limb
because he boasted that his prowess in the hunt surpassed   340
the skill of Artemis.
                                        Do not let his fate be yours.
Here, let me wreathe your head with leaves of ivy.
Then come with us and glorify the god.

PENTHEUS

Take your hands off me! Go worship your Bacchus,
but do not wipe your madness off on me.
By god, I'll make him pay, the man who taught you   345
this folly of yours.

                                                (To his attendants.)

                                Go, someone, this instant,
to the place where this prophet prophesies.
Pry it up with crowbars, heave it over,
upside down; demolish everything you see.
Throw his fillets out to wind and weather.   350
That will provoke him more than anything.

                                (Exit an attendant to one side.)

As for you others, go and scour the city
for that effeminate stranger, the man who infects our women
with this new disease and pollutes their beds.

And if you catch him, clap him in chains   355
and march him here. He shall die as he deserves—
by being stoned to death. He shall come to rue
his merrymaking here in Thebes.

(Exit other attendants to the other side.)

TEIRESIAS

                         Reckless fool,
you do not know the meaning of what you say.
You were out of your mind before, but this is raving
lunacy!

                         Cadmus, let us go and pray   360
for this crazed fool and for this city too,
pray to the god that he take no vengeance
upon us.

                         Take your staff and follow me.
Support me with your hands, and I shall help you too
lest we stumble and fall, a sight of shame,
two old men together.

                         But go we must,   365
acknowledging the service that we owe to god,
Bacchus, the son of Zeus.

                         And yet take care
lest someday your house repent of Pentheus
for its sufferings. I speak not prophecy
but fact. The words of fools finish in folly.

(Exit Teiresias and Cadmus to the side.)

CHORUS [*singing*]

STROPHE A

Holiness, queen of heaven,   370
   Holiness on golden wing
   who fly over the earth,
   do you hear what Pentheus says?
   Do you hear his blasphemy
   against the prince of the blessèd,   375

the god of garlands and banquets,
Bromius, Semele's son?
These blessings he gave:
the sacred company's dance and song,
laughter to the pipe   380
and the loosing of cares
when the shining wine is poured
at the feast for the gods,
and the wine bowl casts its sleep   385
on feasters crowned with ivy.

A tongue without reins,
    defiance, unwisdom—
    their end is disaster.
    But the life of quiet good,
    the wisdom that accepts—   390
    these abide unshaken,
    preserving, sustaining
    the houses of men.
    Far in the air of heaven,
    the sons of heaven live.
    But they watch the lives of men.
    And what passes for wisdom is not;   395
    unwise those who outrange mortal limits.
    Briefly, we live. Wherefore
    he who hunts great things
    may lose his harvest here and now.
    I say: such men are mad,   400
    their counsels evil.

O let me go to Cyprus,
    island of Aphrodite,
    home of the Loves that cast
    their spells on the hearts of men!   405

Or Paphos where the hundred-
mouthed barbarian river
brings ripeness without rain!
To loveliest Pieria, haunt of the Muses,   410
the holy hill of Olympus!
O Bromius, leader, god of joy,
Bromius, take me there!
There the lovely Graces are,
and there Desire, and there
the bacchants have the right to worship.   415

ANTISTROPHE B

The deity, the son of Zeus,
in feast, in festival, delights.
He loves the goddess Peace,
generous of good,
preserver of the young.   420
To rich and poor he gives
the painless delight of wine.
But him he hates who scoffs
at the happiness of those
for whom the day is blessed   425
and blessed the night;
whose simple wisdom shuns the thoughts°
of proud, uncommon men.
What the common people   430
believe and do,
I too believe and do.

(Enter Dionysus from the side, led captive by several attendants.)

ATTENDANT

Pentheus, here we are; not empty-handed either.
We captured the quarry you sent us out to catch.   435
Our prey here was quite tame: refused to run,
but just held out his hands as willing as you please,

completely unafraid. His wine-red cheeks were flushed
and did not pale at all. He stood there smiling,
telling us to rope his hands and march him here.   440
That made things easy—and it made me feel ashamed.
"Listen, stranger," I said, "I am not to blame.
We act under orders from Pentheus. He ordered
your arrest."

        As for those bacchants you clapped in chains
and sent to the prison, they're gone, clean away,   445
went skipping off to the fields crying on their god
Bromius. The chains on their legs snapped apart
by themselves. Untouched by any human hand,
the doors swung wide, opening of their own accord.
Sir, this stranger who has come to Thebes is full   450
of many miracles. I know no more than that.
The rest is your affair.

PENTHEUS

        Untie his hands.
We have him in our net. He may be quick,
but he cannot escape us now, I think.

                (The attendants do as instructed.)

        So,
you are attractive, stranger, at least to women—
which explains, I think, your presence here in Thebes.
Your curls are long; they fall along your cheeks.
You do not wrestle, I take it. And what fair skin!   455
You must take care of it—not in the sun, by night
when you hunt Aphrodite with your beauty.
        Now then,
what country do you come from?

DIONYSUS

        It is nothing   460
to boast of and easily told. You have heard, I suppose,
of Mount Tmolus and her flowers?

PENTHEUS

        I know of the place.
It rings the city of Sardis.

DIONYSUS

        I come from there.
My country is Lydia.

PENTHEUS

        And from where comes this cult
you have imported into Hellas?

DIONYSUS

        Dionysus, the son of Zeus.   465
He initiated me.

PENTHEUS

        You have some local Zeus there
who spawns new gods?

DIONYSUS

        He is the same as yours:
the Zeus who married Semele.

PENTHEUS

        How did you see him?
In a dream or face to face?

DIONYSUS

        Face to face.
He gave me his rites.

PENTHEUS

        What form do they take,   470
these rituals of yours?

DIONYSUS

        It is forbidden
to tell the uninitiate.

PENTHEUS

> Tell me the benefits
that those who know your mysteries enjoy.

DIONYSUS

You're not allowed to hear. But they are worth knowing.

PENTHEUS

Your answers are designed to make me curious.

DIONYSUS

> No: 475
our mysteries abhor an unbelieving man.

PENTHEUS

You say you saw the god. What form did he assume?

DIONYSUS

Whatever form he wished. The choice was his,
not mine.

PENTHEUS

> You evade the question.

DIONYSUS

> Talk sense to a fool
and he calls you foolish.

PENTHEUS

> Have you introduced your rites   480
in other cities too? Or is Thebes the first?

DIONYSUS

Barbarians everywhere now dance for Dionysus.

PENTHEUS

They are more ignorant than Greeks.

DIONYSUS

> In this matter
they are not. Customs differ.

PENTHEUS

                        Do you hold your rites
during the day or night?

DIONYSUS

                        Mostly by night.   485
The darkness is well suited to devotion.

PENTHEUS

Better suited to lechery and seducing women.

DIONYSUS

You can find debauchery by daylight too.

PENTHEUS

You shall regret these clever answers.

DIONYSUS

                        And you,
your stupid blasphemies.

PENTHEUS

                        What a bold bacchant!   490
You wrestle well—when it comes to words.

DIONYSUS

                        Tell me,
what punishment do you propose?

PENTHEUS

                        First of all,
I shall cut off your girlish curls.

DIONYSUS

                        My hair is holy.
My curls belong to god.

(Pentheus shears away some of the god's curls.)

PENTHEUS

                        Second, you will surrender
your wand.

DIONYSUS

You take it. It belongs to Dionysus.   495

(Pentheus takes the thyrsus.)

PENTHEUS

Last, I shall place you under guard and confine you
in the palace.

DIONYSUS

The god himself will set me free
whenever I wish.

PENTHEUS

You will be with your women in prison
when you call on him for help.

DIONYSUS

He is here now
and sees what I endure from you.

PENTHEUS

Where is he?   500
My eyes don't see him.

DIONYSUS

With me. Your blasphemies
have made you blind.

PENTHEUS   (To attendants.)
Seize him. He is mocking me
and Thebes.

DIONYSUS

And I say, Don't chain me up! I am sane
but you are not.

PENTHEUS

But I say: chain him.
And I'm the ruler here.

DIONYSUS

                    You do not know   505
what is the life you live.° You do not know
what you do. You do not know who you are.

PENTHEUS

I am Pentheus, the son of Echion and Agave.

DIONYSUS

Pentheus: you shall repent that name.

PENTHEUS

                    Off with him.
Chain his hands; lock him in the stables by the palace.
Since he desires the darkness, give him what he wants.   510
Let him dance down there in the dark.
                    As for these women,
your accomplices in making trouble here,
I shall have them sold as slaves or put to work
at my looms. That will silence their drums.

DIONYSUS

                    I go,   515
for I won't suffer what I'm not meant to suffer.
But Dionysus whom you outrage by your acts,
who you deny is god, will call you to account.
You mistreat me—but it's he you drag to prison.

        (*Exit Pentheus, Dionysus, and attendants into the palace.*)

CHORUS [*singing*]

                    STROPHE

O Dirce, holy river,   520
    child of Achelous' water,
    yours the springs that welcomed once
    divinity, the son of Zeus!
    For Zeus his father snatched him in his thigh
    from deathless flame, crying: 525

Dithyrambus, come!
Enter my male womb.
I name you, Bacchius, and to Thebes
proclaim you by that name.
But now, O blessed Dirce,   530
you spurn me when to your banks I come,
crowned with ivy, bringing revels.
O Dirce, why do you reject me? Why do you flee me?
By the clustered grapes I swear,
by Dionysus' wine,   535
someday you shall come to know
                the worship of Bromius!

ANTISTROPHE

Pentheus, son of Echion,°   540
        shows he was born of the breed of Earth,
        spawned by the dragon, whelped by Earth,
        inhuman, a rabid beast,
        a Giant in wildness,
        defying the children of heaven.
        He will fetter me soon,   545
        me, who belong to Bromius!
        He cages my comrades with chains;
        he has cast them in prison darkness.
        O lord, son of Zeus, do you see?   550
        O Dionysus, do you see
        how your spokesmen are wrestling with compulsion?
        Descend from Olympus, lord!
        Come, whirl your wand of gold
        and quell the violence of this murderous man!   555

EPODE

O lord, where do you brandish your wand
        among the holy companies?
        There on Nysa, mother of beasts?
        There on the ridges of Corycia?
        Or there among the forests of Olympus   560

where Orpheus fingered his lyre
and mustered with music the trees,
mustered the wilderness beasts?
O Pieria, you are blessed! 565
Euhius honors you. He will come to dance,
bringing his Bacchae, crossing the swift rivers
Axios and Lydias, 570
generous father of wealth
and famed, I hear, for his lovely waters
that fatten a land of good horses. 575

(In the following scene, sounds of thunder, lightning,
and earthquake are heard from offstage.)

DIONYSUS [*singing from within in this lyric interchange with the*
Chorus, who sing in reply]
    Ho!
    Hear me! Ho, Bacchae!
    Ho, Bacchae! Hear my cry!

CHORUS
    Who cries?
    Who calls me with that cry
    of Euhius?

DIONYSUS
    Ho! Again I cry— 580
    I, the son of Zeus and Semele!

CHORUS
    O lord, lord Bromius!
    Bromius, come to our holy company now!

DIONYSUS
    Let the earthquake come! Shatter° the floor of the world! 585

CHORUS
    Look there, soon the palace of Pentheus will totter.
    Dionysus is within. Adore him!

We adore him! 590
Look there!
   Above the pillars, how the great stones
  gape and crack!
   Listen. Bromius cries his victory!

DIONYSUS

Launch the blazing thunderbolt of god!
Consume with flame the palace of Pentheus! 595

CHORUS

Ah,
look how the fire leaps up
on the holy tomb of Semele,
the flame of Zeus of Thunders,
his lightnings, still alive!
Down, maenads, 600
throw to the ground your trembling bodies!
Our lord attacks this palace,
turns it upside down,
the son of Zeus!

     (The Chorus falls to the ground in terror and
     veneration. Enter Dionysus from the palace.)

DIONYSUS [*speaking*]

What's this, women of Asia? So overcome with fright
that you fell to the ground? I think you must have heard 605
how Bacchius jostled the palace of Pentheus. But come, rise.°
Do not be afraid.

CHORUS LEADER

    O greatest light of our holy revels,
how glad I am to see your face! Without you I was lost.

DIONYSUS

Did you despair when they led me away to cast me down 610
in the darkness of Pentheus' prison?

CHORUS LEADER

What else could I do?
Where would I turn for help if something happened to you?
But how did you escape that godless man?

DIONYSUS

No problem.
I saved myself with ease.

CHORUS LEADER

But the manacles on your wrists?   615

DIONYSUS

There I, in turn, humiliated him, outrage for outrage.
He seemed to think that he was chaining me but never once
so much as touched my hands. He fed upon his hopes.
Inside the stable he intended as my jail, instead of me,
he found a bull and tried to rope its knees and hooves.
He was panting desperately, biting his lips with his teeth,   620
his whole body drenched with sweat, while I sat nearby,
quietly watching. But at that moment Bacchus came,
shook the palace and lit his mother's grave with tongues
of fire. Imagining the palace was in flames,
Pentheus went rushing here and there, shouting to his slaves   625
to bring him water. Every hand was put to work: in vain.
Then, afraid I had escaped, he suddenly stopped short,
drew his sword and rushed to the palace. There, it seems,
Bromius had made a phantom—at least it seemed to me—   630
within the court. Pursuing, Pentheus thrust and stabbed
at that thing of gleaming air° as though he were killing me.
And then, once again, Bacchius humiliated him.
He razed the palace to the ground where it lies, shattered
in utter ruin—his reward for my imprisonment.
At that bitter sight, Pentheus dropped his sword, exhausted   635
by the struggle. A man, a man, and nothing more,
yet he presumed to wage a war with god.

For my part,
I left the palace quietly and made my way outside.
For Pentheus I care nothing.

But judging from the sound
of tramping feet inside the court, I think our man
will soon come out. What, I wonder, will he have to say?   640
But let him bluster. I shall not be touched to rage.
Wise men know constraint: our passions are controlled.

(Enter Pentheus from the palace.)

PENTHEUS

What has happened to me is monstrous! That stranger, that
    man
I clapped in irons, has escaped.

(He catches sight of Dionysus.)

What! You?   645
Well, what do you have to say for yourself?
How did you escape? Answer me.

DIONYSUS

Your anger
walks too heavily. Tread lightly here.

PENTHEUS

How did you escape?

DIONYSUS

Don't you remember?
Someone, I said, would set me free.

PENTHEUS

Someone?   650
But who? The things you say are always strange.

DIONYSUS

He who makes the grape grow its clusters
for mankind.

PENTHEUS

His chiefest glory is his reproach.°

DIONYSUS

The god himself will come to teach you wisdom.

PENTHEUS

I hereby order every gate in every tower
to be bolted tight.

(Exit some attendants to the sides.)

DIONYSUS

And so? Could not a god
hurdle your city walls?

PENTHEUS

You are clever—very—   655
but not where it counts.

DIONYSUS

Where it counts the most,
there I am clever.

(Enter a herdsman as Messenger from the side.)

But hear this messenger
who brings you news from the mountain of Cithaeron.
I shall remain where we are. Do not fear:
I will not run away.

MESSENGER

Pentheus, king of Thebes,   660
I come from Cithaeron where the gleaming flakes of snow
fall on and on forever.

PENTHEUS

Get to the point.
What is your message, man?

MESSENGER

Sir, I have seen

the holy maenads, the women who ran barefoot 665
and crazy from the city, and I wanted to report
to you and Thebes what strange fantastic things,
what miracles and more than miracles,
these women do. But may I speak freely
of what happened there, or should I trim my words?
I fear the harsh impatience of your nature, sire, 670
too kingly and too quick to anger.

PENTHEUS

    Speak freely.
You have my promise: I shall not punish you.
Displeasure with a man of justice is not right.°
However, the more terrible this tale of yours,
that much more terrible will be the punishment 675
I impose upon this man who taught our womenfolk
these strange new skills.

MESSENGER

    About that hour
when the sun sends forth its light to warm the earth,
our grazing herds of cows had just begun to climb
the path along the mountain ridge. Suddenly
I saw three companies of women dancers, 680
one led by Autonoë, the second captained
by your mother Agave, while Ino led the third.
There they lay in the deep sleep of exhaustion,
some resting on boughs of fir, others sleeping
where they fell, here and there among the oak leaves— 685
but all modestly and soberly, not, as you think,
drunk with wine, nor wandering, led astray
by the music of the pipe, to hunt their Aphrodite
through the woods.

    But your mother heard the lowing
of our hornèd herds, and springing to her feet, 690
gave a great cry to waken them from sleep.
And they too, rubbing the bloom of deep sleep

from their eyes, rose up lightly and straight—
a lovely sight to see: all together in fine order,
the old women and the young and the unmarried girls.
First they let their hair fall loose, down   695
over their shoulders, and those whose fastenings had slipped
closed up their skins of fawn with writhing snakes
that licked their cheeks. Breasts swollen with milk,
new mothers who had left their babies behind at home
nestled gazelles and young wolves in their arms,   700
suckling them. Then they crowned their hair with leaves,
ivy and oak and flowering bryony. One woman
struck her thyrsus against a rock and a fountain
of cool water came bubbling up. Another drove   705
her fennel in the ground, and where it struck the earth,
at the god's touch, a spring of wine poured out.
Those who wanted milk scratched at the soil
with bare fingers and the white milk came welling up.   710
Pure honey spurted, streaming, from their wands.
If you had been there and seen these wonders for yourself,
you'd surely yourself have approached with fervent prayers
the god you now deny.
                    We cowherds and shepherds
gathered together, wondering and arguing   715
among ourselves at these fantastic things,
the awesome miracles those women did.°
But then a city fellow with the knack of words
rose to his feet and said: "All you who live
upon the pastures of the mountain, what do you say?
Shall we earn a little favor with King Pentheus   720
by hunting his mother Agave out of the revels?"
Falling in with his suggestion, we withdrew
and set ourselves in ambush, hidden by the leaves
among the undergrowth. At the appointed time
the bacchants began to shake their wands in worship
of Bacchus. With one voice they cried aloud:
"O Iacchus! Son of Zeus!" "O Bromius!" they cried   725

until the beasts and all the mountain were
wild with divinity. And when they ran,
everything ran with them.

           It happened, however,
that Agave ran near the ambush where I lay
concealed. Leaping up, I tried to seize her,   730
but she gave a cry: "Hounds who run with me,
men are hunting us down! Follow, follow me!
Use your wands for weapons."

           At this we fled
and barely escaped being torn to pieces by the women.
Unarmed, they swooped down upon the herds of cattle   735
grazing there on the green of the meadow. And then
you could have seen a single woman with bare hands
tear a fat calf, still bellowing with fright,
in two, while others clawed the heifers to pieces.
There were ribs and cloven hooves scattered everywhere,   740
and scraps smeared with blood hung from the fir trees.
And bulls, their raging fury gathered in their horns,
lowered their heads to charge, then fell, stumbling
to the earth, pulled down by hordes of women   745
and stripped of flesh and skin more quickly, sire,
than you could blink your royal eyes. Then,
carried up by their own speed, they flew like birds
across the spreading fields along Asopus' stream
where the rich soil yields plentiful grain for Thebes.   750
Like invaders they swooped on Hysiae
and on Erythrae in the foothills of Cithaeron.
Everything in sight they pillaged and destroyed.
They snatched the children from their homes. And see —
    whatever
they piled as plunder on their shoulders stayed in place,   755
untied. Nothing, neither bronze nor iron,
fell to the dark earth.° They were carrying fire
in their hair — it did not burn them. Then the villagers,
furious at what the Bacchae did, took to arms.

And there, sire, was something terrible to see.   760
For the men's spears were pointed and sharp, and yet
drew no blood, whereas the wands the women threw
inflicted wounds. And then the men ran,
routed by women! Some god, I say, was with them.
The women then returned where they had started,   765
by the springs the god had made, and washed their hands
while the snakes licked away the drops of blood
that dabbled their cheeks.

    Whoever this god may be,
sire, welcome him to Thebes. For he is great
in many ways, but above all it was he,   770
or so they say, who gave to mortal men
the gift of lovely wine by which our suffering
is stopped. And if there is no god of wine,
there is no love, no Aphrodite either,
nor other pleasure left to men.

         (Exit Messenger to the side.)

CHORUS LEADER
        I tremble   775
to speak my words in freedom before a tyrant.
But nonetheless I'll say: there is no god
greater than Dionysus.

PENTHEUS
        Like a blazing fire
this Bacchic violence spreads. It comes too close.
We are disgraced, humiliated in the eyes
of Hellas. This is no time for hesitation.   780

         (To an attendant.)

You there. Go down quickly to the Electran gates
and order out all heavy-armored infantry;
call up the fastest troops among our cavalry,
the mobile squadrons and the archers. We'll march

against the Bacchae! Affairs are out of hand   785
if we tamely endure such conduct in our women.

> *(Exit attendant to the side.)*

DIONYSUS

Pentheus, you seem to hear, and yet you disregard
my words of warning. You have done me wrong,
and yet, in spite of that, I warn you once
again: do not take arms against a god.
Stay quiet here. Bromius will not let you   790
drive his women from their worship on the mountains.

PENTHEUS

Don't you lecture me. You escaped from prison.
Or shall I punish you again?

DIONYSUS

                                     If I were you,
I would offer him a sacrifice, not rage
and kick against necessity, a man defying   795
god.

PENTHEUS

        I shall give your god the sacrifice
that he deserves: the blood of those same women.
I shall make a great slaughter in the woods of Cithaeron.

DIONYSUS

You will all be routed, shamefully defeated,
when their wands of ivy turn back your shields
of bronze.

PENTHEUS

                  Impossible to wrestle with this foreigner!   800
Whether he's victim or culprit, he won't hold his tongue.

DIONYSUS

                         Friend,
you can still save the situation.

PENTHEUS

How?
By accepting orders from my own slaves?

DIONYSUS

No.
I undertake to lead the women back to Thebes.
Without weapons.

PENTHEUS

This is some trap.

DIONYSUS

A trap?   805
How so, if I save you by my own devices?

PENTHEUS

I know.
You and they have agreed to establish your rites
forever.

DIONYSUS

True, I've agreed to this—with the god.

PENTHEUS

Bring my armor, someone. And you—stop talking!   810

DIONYSUS

Wait!
Would you like to see them sitting on the mountains?

PENTHEUS

I would pay a lot of gold to see that sight.

DIONYSUS

What? Are you so passionately curious?

PENTHEUS

Of course
I'd be sorry to see them drunk.

DIONYSUS

But for all your pain,   815
you'd be very glad to see it?

PENTHEUS

Yes, very much.
I could crouch beneath the fir trees, quietly.

DIONYSUS

But if you try to hide, they will track you down.

PENTHEUS

Your point is well taken. I will go openly.

DIONYSUS

Shall I lead you there now? Are you ready to go?

PENTHEUS

The sooner the better. I want no delay!   820

DIONYSUS

Then you must dress yourself in women's clothes.

PENTHEUS

Why?
I'm a man. You want me to become a woman?

DIONYSUS

If they see that you're a man, they'll kill you instantly.

PENTHEUS

True. You are an old hand at cunning, I see.

DIONYSUS

Dionysus taught me everything I know.   825

PENTHEUS

How can we arrange to follow your advice?

DIONYSUS

I'll go inside with you and help you dress.

PENTHEUS

In a woman's dress, you mean? I'd be ashamed.

DIONYSUS

Then you no longer hanker to see the maenads?

PENTHEUS

What is this costume I must wear?

DIONYSUS

On your head   830
I shall make your hair long and luxuriant.

PENTHEUS

And then?

DIONYSUS

Next, robes to your feet and a headband for your hair.

PENTHEUS

Yes? Go on.

DIONYSUS

Then a thyrsus for your hand
and a skin of dappled fawn.

PENTHEUS

I could not bear it.   835
I cannot bring myself to dress in women's clothes.

DIONYSUS

Then you must fight the Bacchae. That means bloodshed.

PENTHEUS

Right. First we must go and reconnoiter.

DIONYSUS

Surely a wiser course than that of hunting bad
with worse.

PENTHEUS

But how can I pass through the city
without being seen?

DIONYSUS

         We shall take deserted streets. 840

I will lead the way.

PENTHEUS

         It's all fine with me,

provided those women of Bacchus don't jeer at me.

First, however, I shall ponder your advice,°

whether to go or not.

DIONYSUS

         Do as you please.

I am ready, whatever you decide.

PENTHEUS

        I'll go in.

Either I shall march with my army to the mountain 845

or act on your advice.

        (Exit Pentheus into the palace.)

DIONYSUS

        Women, our prey is walking

into the net we threw. He shall see the Bacchae

and pay the price with death.

        O Dionysus,

now action rests with you. And you are near.

Punish this man. But first distract his wits; 850

bewilder him with madness. For sane of mind

this man would never wear a woman's dress;

but obsess his soul and he will not refuse.

After those threats with which he was so fierce,

I want him made the laughingstock of Thebes,

led through the town in woman's form.

        But now 855

I shall go and costume Pentheus in the clothes

which he will wear to Hades when he dies, butchered

by the hands of his mother. He shall come to know

Dionysus, son of Zeus, consummate god, 860
most terrible, and yet most gentle, to humankind.

(*Exit Dionysus into the palace.*)

CHORUS [*singing*]

STROPHE

When shall I dance once more
  with bare feet the all-night dances,
  tossing my head for joy
  in the damp air, in the dew, 865
  as a running fawn would frisk
  for the green joy of the wide fields,
  freed from fear of the hunt,
  freed from the circling beaters 870
  and the nets of woven mesh
  and the hunters hallooing on
  their yelping packs? And then, hard pressed,
  she sprints with the quickness of wind,
  bounding over the marsh,
    leaping for joy by the river, 875
  joyous at the green of the leaves,
    where no man is.
What is wisdom? What gift of the gods°
  is held in honor like this:
  to hold your hand victorious
  over the heads of those you hate? 880
  Honor is cherished forever.

ANTISTROPHE

Slow but unmistakable
  the might of the gods moves.
  It punishes that man
  who honors folly
  and with mad conceit 885
  disregards the gods.
  The gods are crafty:

they lie in ambush
a long step of time
to hunt the unholy. 890
Beyond the old beliefs,
no thought, no act shall go.
Small, small is the cost
to believe in this:
whatever is god is strong,
whatever long time has sanctioned, 895
and the law of nature.
What is wisdom? What gift of the gods°
is held in honor like this:
to hold your hand victorious
over the heads of those you hate? 900
Honor is cherished forever.

EPODE

Blessed is he who escapes a storm at sea,
who comes home to his harbor.
Blessed is he who emerges from under affliction.
In various ways one man outraces another in the
race for wealth and power. 905
Ten thousand men possess ten thousand hopes.
A few bear fruit in happiness; the others go awry.
But he who garners day by day a happy life, 910
him I call truly blessed.

(Enter Dionysus from the palace.)

DIONYSUS

Pentheus! If you are still so curious to see
and do forbidden sights, forbidden things,
come out. Let us see you in your woman's dress,
disguised in maenad clothes so you may go and spy 915
upon your mother and her company.

(Enter Pentheus from the palace, dressed as a
bacchant and carrying a thyrsus.)

Why,

you look exactly like one of the daughters of Cadmus.

PENTHEUS

I seem to see two suns blazing in the heavens.
And now two Thebes, two cities, and each
with seven gates. And you—you are a bull   920
who walks before me there. Horns have sprouted
from your head. Have you always been a beast?
Well, now you have become a bull.

DIONYSUS

The god

was hostile formerly, but now declares a truce
and goes with us. You now see what you should.

PENTHEUS   (Coyly primping.)

How do I look in my getup? Don't I move like Ino?   925
Or like my mother Agave?

DIONYSUS

So much alike

I think I might be seeing one of them. But look:
one of your curls has come loose from under the band
where I tucked it.

PENTHEUS

It must have worked loose

when I was dancing for joy and tossing my head.   930

DIONYSUS

Then let me assist you now and tuck it back.
Hold still.

PENTHEUS

Arrange it. I am in your hands

completely.

(Dionysus rearranges Pentheus' hair.)

DIONYSUS

       And your strap has slipped. Yes,   935
and your robe hangs askew at the ankles.

PENTHEUS   *(Bending backward to look.)*

       I think so.
At least on my right leg. But on the left the hem
lies straight.

DIONYSUS

       You will think me the best of friends
when you see to your surprise how chaste the Bacchae are.   940

PENTHEUS

But to be a real bacchant, should I hold
the wand in my right hand? Or this way?

DIONYSUS

                No.
In your right hand. And raise it as you raise
your right foot. I commend your change of heart.

PENTHEUS

Could I lift Cithaeron up, do you think?   945
Shoulder the cliffs, Bacchae and all?

DIONYSUS

           If you wanted.
Your mind was once unsound, but now you think
as sane men do.

PENTHEUS

       Should we take crowbars with us?
Or should I put my shoulder to the cliffs   950
and heave them up?

DIONYSUS

       What? And destroy the haunts
of the nymphs, the holy groves where Pan plays
his woodland pipes?

PENTHEUS

You are right. In any case,
women should not be mastered by brute strength.
I will hide myself among the firs instead.

DIONYSUS

You will find all the ambush you deserve,   955
creeping up to spy on the maenads.

PENTHEUS

Think.
I can see them already, there among the bushes,
mating like birds, caught in the toils of love.

DIONYSUS

Exactly. This is your mission: you go to watch.
You may surprise them—or they may surprise you.   960

PENTHEUS

Then lead me through the very heart of Thebes,
since I'm the only one who's man enough to go.

DIONYSUS

You and you alone will labor for your city.
A great ordeal awaits you, the one that you're allotted
as your fate. I shall lead you safely there;   965
someone else shall bring you back . . .

PENTHEUS

Yes, my mother.

DIONYSUS

. . . conspicuous to all men.

PENTHEUS

It is for that I go.

DIONYSUS

You will be carried home . . .

PENTHEUS

O luxury!

DIONYSUS

. . . cradled in your mother's arms.

PENTHEUS

You will spoil me!

DIONYSUS

Yes, in a certain way.

PENTHEUS

I go to my reward.   970

DIONYSUS

You are an extraordinary young man, and you go
to an extraordinary experience. You shall win
fame high as heaven.

Agave, Cadmus' daughters,°
reach out your hands! I bring this young man
to a great contest, where I shall be the victor,   975
I—and Bromius. The rest the event shall show.

(Exit Dionysus to the side, followed by Pentheus.)

CHORUS [*singing*]

STROPHE

Run to the mountain, fleet hounds of madness!
   Run, run to the holy company of Cadmus' daughters!
   Sting them against the man in women's clothes,   980
   the madman who spies on the maenads!
   From behind the rocks, keen-sighted,
   his mother shall see him spying first.
   She will cry to the maenads: 985
   "Who is this who has come
   to the mountains to peer at the mountain revels
   of the women of Thebes?
   Who bore him, Bacchae?

This man was born of no woman. Some lioness
gave him birth, some Libyan Gorgon!"   990
O Justice,
    come! Be manifest; reveal yourself with a sword!
    Stab through the throat that godless, lawless, unjust man,
        the earth-born spawn of Echion!   995

ANTISTROPHE

Uncontrollable, the unbeliever goes,°
    in spitting rage, rebellious and amok,
    madly assaulting Bacchus' mysteries and his mother's.
    Against the unassailable he runs, with rage   1000
    obsessed. But death will chastise his ideas.°
    To accept the gods, to act as a mortal—
    that is a life free from pain.
    I do not resent wisdom and I rejoice to hunt it.   1005
    But other things are great and clear
    and make life beautiful:
    purity, piety, day into night,
    honoring the gods,
    rejecting customs outside justice.   1010
O Justice,
    come! Be manifest; reveal yourself with a sword!
    Stab through the throat that godless, lawless, unjust man,
        the earth-born spawn of Echion!   1015

EPODE

O Dionysus, reveal yourself a bull! Be manifest,
    a snake with darting heads, a lion breathing fire!
    O Bacchus, go! Go with your smile!
    Cast your deadly noose about this man who hunts
    your Bacchae! Make him fall   1020
        to your maenad throng!

(Enter from the side a servant of Pentheus as a second Messenger.)

MESSENGER

How prosperous in Hellas these halls once were,

this house founded by Cadmus, the old man from Sidon°   1025
who sowed the earth-born crop of the dragon snake!
I am a slave and nothing more, yet even so
I mourn the fortunes of this fallen house.°

CHORUS LEADER
                    What is it?
Is there news from the Bacchae?

MESSENGER
                    This is my news:
Pentheus, the son of Echion, is dead.   1030

CHORUS [singing and continuing to sing in the following]
All hail to Bromius! Our god is a great god!

MESSENGER
What is this you say, woman? You dare to rejoice
at these disasters which destroy this house?

CHORUS
I am no Greek. I hail my god
in barbarian song. No longer need I
shrink with fear of prison.   1035

MESSENGER
If you suppose this city is so short of men ...°

CHORUS
Dionysus, Dionysus, not Thebes,
has power over me.

MESSENGER
Your feelings might be forgiven, then. But this,
your exultation in disaster—it is not right.   1040

CHORUS
Tell us how that lawless man died.
How was he killed?

There were three of us in all: Pentheus and I,
attending my master, and that stranger who volunteered
to guide us to the show. Leaving behind us
the last outlying farms of Thebes, we forded
the Asopus and struck into the barren scrubland   1045
of Cithaeron.

            There in a grassy glen we halted,
unmoving, silent, without a word,
so we might see but not be seen. From that vantage,   1050
in a steep meadow along the sheer rock of the cliffs,
a place where water ran and the pines grew dense
with shade, we saw the maenads sitting, their hands
busily moving at their happy tasks. Some
wound the stalks of their tattered wands with tendrils   1055
of fresh ivy; others, frisking like fillies
newly freed from the painted bridles, chanted
in Bacchic songs, responsively.

            But Pentheus—
unhappy man—could not quite see the companies
of women. "Stranger," he said, "from where we stand,
I cannot see these counterfeited maenads.°   1060
But if I climbed that towering fir that overhangs
the banks, then I could see their shameless orgies
better."

            And now the stranger worked a miracle.
Reaching for the highest branch of the great fir,
he bent it down, down, down to the dark earth,   1065
till it was curved the way a taut bow bends
or like a rim of wood when forced about the circle
of a wheel. Like that he forced that mountain fir
down to the ground. No mortal could have done it.
Then he seated Pentheus at the highest tip   1070
and with his hands let the trunk rise straightly up,
slowly and gently, lest it throw its rider.
And the tree rose, towering to heaven, with my master

seated at the top. And now the maenads saw him
more clearly than he saw them. But barely had they seen,   1075
when the stranger vanished and there came a great voice
out of heaven—Dionysus', it must have been—
crying: "Women, I bring you the man who mocks
at you and me and at our holy mysteries.   1080
Take vengeance upon him." And as he spoke
a flash of awful fire bound earth and heaven.

    The high air hushed, and along the forest glen
the leaves hung still; you could hear no cry of beasts.   1085
The Bacchae heard that voice but missed its words,
and leaping up, they stared, peering everywhere.
Again that voice. And now they knew his cry,
the clear command of Bacchius. Breaking loose
like startled doves,° through grove and torrent,   1090
over rocks, the Bacchae flew, their feet maddened
by the god's breath. And when they saw my master
perching on his tree, they climbed a great rock   1095
that towered opposite his perch and showered him
with stones and branches of fir, while the others
hurled their wands. What grim target practice!
But they didn't hit Pentheus, barely out of reach   1100
of their eager hands, treed, unable to escape.
Finally they splintered branches from the oaks
and with those bars of wood tried to lever up the tree
by prying at the roots. But every effort failed.   1105
Then Agave cried out: "Maenads, make a circle
about the trunk and grip it with your hands.
Unless we take this climbing beast, he will reveal
the secrets of the god." With that, thousands of hands
tore the fir tree from the earth, and down, down   1110
from his high perch fell Pentheus, tumbling
to the ground, sobbing and screaming as he fell,
for he knew his end was near.
              His own mother,
like a priestess with her victim, fell upon him

first. But snatching from his hair the headband   1115
so poor Agave would recognize and spare him, he said,
touching her cheeks, "No, Mother! I am Pentheus,
your own son, the child you bore to Echion!
Pity me, spare me, Mother! I have done a wrong,   1120
but do not kill your own son for that offense."
But she was foaming at the mouth, and her crazed eyes
rolled with frenzy. She was mad, stark mad,
possessed by Bacchus. Ignoring his cries of pity,
she seized his left arm at the wrist; then, planting   1125
her foot upon his chest, she pulled, wrenching away
the arm at the shoulder—not by her own strength,
for the god had put inhuman power in her hands.
Ino, meanwhile, on the other side, was scratching off
his flesh. Then Autonoë and the whole horde   1130
of Bacchae swarmed upon him. Shouts everywhere—
him groaning with what little breath was left,
them shrieking in triumph. One bore off an arm,
another a foot still warm in its shoe. His ribs
were clawed clean of flesh and every hand   1135
was smeared with blood as they played ball with scraps
of Pentheus' body.

        The pitiful remains lie scattered,
one piece among the sharp rocks, others
among the leaves in the deep woods—not easy
to search for. His mother, picking up his head,   1140
impaled it on her wand. She seems to think it is
some mountain lion's head which she carries in triumph
through the thick of Cithaeron. Leaving her sisters
at the maenad dances, she is coming here, gloating
over her grisly prize. She calls upon Bacchius: 1145
he is her "fellow huntsman," "comrade of the chase,"
"crowned with victory." But all the victory
she carries home is her own grief.

        Now,
before Agave returns, I shall leave

this scene of sorrow. Humility,
a sense of reverence before the sons of heaven—   1150
of all the prizes that a mortal man might win,
these, I say, are wisest; these are best.

(Exit Messenger to the side.)

CHORUS [*singing*]
Let us dance to the glory of Bacchius,
      dance to the death of Pentheus,
      the death of the spawn of the dragon!   1155
      He dressed in woman's dress;
      he took the lovely thyrsus;
      it waved him down to death,°
            led by a bull to Hades.
      Hail, Bacchae of Thebes!   1160
      Your victory is fair, fair the prize,
            this famous prize of grief, of tears!
      Glorious the game, to fold your child
      in your arms, streaming with his blood!

(Enter Agave from the side carrying the head of
Pentheus impaled upon her thyrsus.)

CHORUS LEADER
But look: here comes Pentheus' mother, Agave,   1165
running wild-eyed toward the palace.
                              Welcome,
welcome to the reveling band of the god of joy!

AGAVE [*singing in this lyric interchange with the Chorus, who sing in
reply*]

STROPHE

Bacchae of Asia . . .

CHORUS
Tell me.

AGAVE
. . . *we bring this branch to the palace,*

this fresh-cut tendril from the mountains. 1170
Happy was the hunting.

CHORUS

                              I see.
I welcome our fellow-reveler.

AGAVE

The cub of a wild mountain lion,°
and snared by me without a noose—
look, look! 1175

CHORUS

Where was he caught?

AGAVE

                            Cithaeron . . .

CHORUS

Cithaeron?

AGAVE

                      . . . killed him.

CHORUS

Who struck him?

AGAVE

                   The first honor is mine.
The maenads call me "Agave the blest." 1180

CHORUS

And then who?

AGAVE

             Cadmus' . . .

CHORUS

                Cadmus'?

AGAVE

                   . . . daughters.

After me, they hit the prey.
After me. Happy was their hunting.

ANTISTROPHE

Share the feast!

CHORUS

            Share, unhappy woman?

AGAVE

See, the cub is young and tender.   1185
Beneath the soft mane of hair,
the down is blooming on the cheeks.

CHORUS

Yes, that mane does look like a wild beast's.

AGAVE

Our god is wise. Cunningly, cleverly,   1190
Bacchius the hunter lashed the maenads
against his prey.

CHORUS

            Our king is a hunter.

AGAVE

Do you praise?

CHORUS

            Yes, I praise.

AGAVE

The men of Thebes soon . . .

CHORUS

            . . . and Pentheus, your son . . .

AGAVE

. . . will praise his mother. She caught   1195
a great quarry, this lion's cub.

CHORUS
   Extraordinary catch.

AGAVE
                    Extraordinary skill.

CHORUS
   You are proud?

AGAVE
                    Proud and happy.
   I have won the trophy of the chase,
   a great prize, manifest to all.

CHORUS LEADER [*speaking*]
   Then, poor woman, show the citizens of Thebes   1200
   this great prize, this trophy you have won
   in the hunt.

AGAVE [*speaking*]
                    You citizens of this towered city,
   men of Thebes, behold the trophy of your women's
   hunting! This is the quarry of our chase, taken
   not with nets nor Thessalian spears but by   1205
   the dainty hands of women. What are they worth,
   your javelins now and all that uselessness
   your armor is, since we, with our bare hands,
   captured this quarry and tore its bleeding body
   limb from limb?
                    But where is my old father, Cadmus?   1210
   He should come. And my son. Where is Pentheus?
   Fetch him. I will have him set his ladder up
   against the wall and, there upon the beam,
   nail the head of this wild lion I have killed
   as a trophy of my hunt.

   (*Enter Cadmus from the side, with attendants bearing a covered bier.*)

CADMUS

Follow me, attendants.   1215
Bear your dreadful burden of Pentheus and set it down
there before the palace.

(The attendants do as instructed.)

Now I bring it,
this body—after long and weary searchings
I painfully gathered it from Cithaeron's glens
where it lay, scattered in shreds, dismembered
throughout the forest, no two pieces   1220
in a single place.°
Old Teiresias and I
had returned to Thebes from the Bacchae on the mountain
before I learned of this atrocious crime
my daughters did. And so I hurried back
to the mountain to recover the body of this boy   1225
murdered by the maenads. There among the oaks
I found Aristaeus' wife, the mother of Actaeon,
Autonoë, and with her Ino, both
still stung with madness. But Agave, they said,
was on her way to Thebes, still possessed.   1230
And what they said was true, for there she is,
and not a happy sight.

AGAVE

Now, Father,
yours can be the proudest boast of living men,
because you are the father of the bravest daughters
in the world. All of your daughters are brave,   1235
but I above the rest. I have left my shuttle
at the loom; I raised my sight to higher things—
to hunting animals with my bare hands.
You see?
Here in my hands I hold the quarry of my chase,
a trophy for our house, to be nailed up high

upon its walls. Come Father, take it in your hands.   1240
Glory in my kill and invite your friends to share
the feast of triumph. For you are blest, Father,
by this great deed we have done.

CADMUS

                              This is a grief°
so great it knows no size. I cannot look.
This is the awful murder your hands have done.   1245
This, this is the noble victim you have slaughtered
to the gods. And to share a feast like this
you now invite all Thebes and me?
                              O gods,
how terribly I pity you and then myself.
Justly—yes, but excessively has lord Bromius,
this god of our own blood, destroyed us all,   1250
every one.

AGAVE

                    How scowling and crabbed is old age
in mortals. I hope my son takes after his mother
and wins, as she has done, the laurels of the chase
when he goes hunting with the younger men of Thebes.
But all my son can do is quarrel with god.   1255
He should be scolded, Father, and you are the one
who should scold him. Yes, someone call him here
so he can see his mother's triumph.

CADMUS

                         Enough. No more.
If you realize the horror you have done,
you shall suffer terribly. But if instead   1260
your present madness lasts until you die,
you'll not seem unhappy, but you won't be happy.

AGAVE

Why do you reproach me? Is there something wrong?

CADMUS

First raise your eyes to the heavens.

AGAVE

There.   1265

But why?

CADMUS

Does it look the same as it did before?
Or has it changed?

AGAVE

It seems—somehow—clearer,
brighter than it was before.

CADMUS

Do you still feel
the same flurry inside you?

AGAVE

The same—flurry?
No, I feel—somehow—calmer. I feel as though—   1270
my mind were somehow—changing.

CADMUS

Can you still hear me?
Can you answer clearly?

AGAVE

Yes. I have forgotten
what we said before, Father.

CADMUS

Who was your husband?

AGAVE

Echion—a man, they said, born of the dragon seed.

CADMUS

What was the name of the child you bore your husband?   1275

AGAVE

Pentheus.

CADMUS

And whose head do you hold in your hands?

AGAVE

A lion's head—or so the hunters told me.

CADMUS

Look directly at it. That's quickly done.

AGAVE

Aah! What is it? What am I holding in my hands?   1280

CADMUS

Look more closely still. Study it carefully.

AGAVE

No! O gods, I see the greatest grief there is.

CADMUS

Does it look like a lion now?

AGAVE

                                     No, no. It is—

Pentheus' head—I hold.

CADMUS

                                   And mourned by me   1285

before you ever knew.

AGAVE

                                  But who killed him?

Why am I holding him?

CADMUS

                                  O savage truth,

what a time to come!

AGAVE

For god's sake, speak.
My heart is beating with terror.

CADMUS

You killed him.
You and your sisters.

AGAVE

But where was he killed?   1290
Here at home? Where?

CADMUS

He was killed on Cithaeron,
there where the hounds tore Actaeon to pieces.

AGAVE

But why? Why had Pentheus gone to Cithaeron?

CADMUS

He went to your revels to mock the god.

AGAVE

But we—
what were we doing on the mountain?

CADMUS

You were mad.   1295
The whole city was possessed.

AGAVE

Now, now I see:
Dionysus has destroyed us all.

CADMUS

You outraged him.
You denied that he was truly god.

AGAVE

Father,
where is my poor boy's body now?

CADMUS

                            There it is.
I gathered the pieces with great difficulty.

AGAVE

Is his body entire? Has he been laid out well?   1300

CADMUS

. . . . °

AGAVE

But how did Pentheus share in my own folly?

CADMUS

He, like you, blasphemed the god. And so
the god has brought us all to ruin at one blow,
you, your sisters, and this boy. All our house
the god has utterly destroyed and, with it,
me. For I have no sons, have no male heir;   1305
and I have lived only to see this boy,
this fruit of your own body, most horribly
and foully killed.

                              (To the corpse.)

                    To you my house looked up.
Child, you were the stay of my house; you were
my daughter's son. Of you this city stood in awe.   1310
No one who once had seen your face dared outrage
the old man, for if he did, you punished him.
Now I must go, a banished and dishonored man—
I, Cadmus the great, who sowed the soldiery
of Thebes and harvested a great harvest. My son,   1315
dearest to me of all men—for even dead,
I count you still the man I love the most—
never again will your hand touch my chin;
no more, child, will you hug me and call me
"Grandfather" and say, "Who is wronging you?   1320
Does anyone trouble you or vex your heart, old man?

Tell me, Grandfather, and I will punish him."
No, now there is grief for me; the mourning
for you; pity for your mother; and for her sisters,
sorrow.

       If there is still any mortal man   1325
who despises or defies divinity, let him look
on this boy's death and believe in the gods.

CHORUS LEADER

Cadmus, I pity you. Your daughter's son
has died as he deserved, and yet his death
bears hard on you.

AGAVE

             O Father, now you can see
how all my life has changed.

. . . . ＊○

DIONYSUS   *(Addressing Cadmus.)*

          You, Cadmus, shall be changed   1330
to a serpent, and your wife, the child of Ares,

---

*At this point there is a break in the manuscript of at least fifty lines. The general outlines of the missing section can be reconstructed as follows: Agave, aware that she is now polluted, asks if she may nonetheless lay her son's corpse out so that she can say farewell to him and he can be buried. Cadmus agrees but warns her of its pitiful state. Leaning over the body, she voices piteous accusations against herself, embracing Pentheus' limbs one by one and mourning over them. Suddenly Dionysus appears above the palace, probably no longer in his human disguise but in his divine splendor, and addresses all those present: He accuses the Thebans, who had denied his divinity and rejected his gift of wine, and especially Pentheus for his many outrages against him. He then foretells the future of each survivor in turn: the descendants of Cadmus will someday be banished from Thebes; Agave and her sisters must immediately be exiled as murderers. Finally the god addresses Cadmus; it is at this point that the manuscript resumes. For the sources used by scholars to reconstruct the missing section, see the textual note on line 1329; see also the introduction to this play. Arrowsmith's own hypothetical version of the missing section is provided in the appendix.

immortal Harmonia, shall undergo your doom,
a serpent too. With her, it is your fate
to make a journey in a cart drawn on by oxen,
leading behind you a huge barbarian host.
For thus decrees the oracle of Zeus.
You shall ravage many cities; but when your army   1335
plunders the shrine of Apollo, its homecoming
shall be wretched and hard. Yet in the end
the god Ares shall save Harmonia and you
and settle you both in the Land of the Blessed.

    So say I, born of no mortal father,   1340
Dionysus, true son of Zeus. If then,
when you would not, you had muzzled your madness
and been self-controlled, you'd all be happy now,
and would have the son of Zeus as your ally.

CADMUS°

We implore you, Dionysus. We have done wrong.

DIONYSUS

Too late. You did not know me when you should have.   1345

CADMUS

We have learned. But you punish us too harshly.

DIONYSUS

I am a god. I was blasphemed by you.

CADMUS

Gods should be exempt from human passions.

DIONYSUS

Long ago my father Zeus ordained these things.

AGAVE

It is fated, Father. We must go.

DIONYSUS

           Why then delay?   1350
For you must go.

CADMUS
        Child, to what a dreadful end
have we all° come, poor you, your wretched sisters,
and my unhappy self. An old man, I must go
to live a stranger among barbarian peoples, doomed   1355
to lead against Hellas a motley barbarian army.
Transformed to serpents, I and my wife,
Harmonia, the child of Ares, we must captain
spearmen against the tombs and shrines of Hellas.
Never shall my sufferings end; not even   1360
in Hades shall I ever have peace.

AGAVE
             O Father,
to be banished, to live without you!

CADMUS
          Poor child,
like a swan embracing its hoary, worn-out father,   1365
why do you clasp your arms about my neck?

AGAVE
But banished! Where shall I go?

CADMUS
          I do not know,
my child. Your father can no longer help you.

AGAVE [chanting]
Farewell, my home! City, farewell.
O bedchamber, banished I go,   1370
in misery, I leave you now.

CADMUS [chanting henceforth]
Go, poor child, to the burial place°
of Aristaeus' son on Cithaeron.

AGAVE [chanting]
I pity you, Father.

CADMUS

                     And I pity you, my child,
and I grieve for your poor sisters. I pity them.

AGAVE [*singing*]
   Terribly has Dionysus brought°   1375
   disaster down upon this house.

CADMUS°
   He was terribly blasphemed by us,
   his name dishonored in Thebes.

AGAVE [*chanting henceforth*]
   Farewell, Father.

CADMUS

                   Farewell to you, unhappy child.
   Fare well. But you shall find your faring hard.   1380

AGAVE
   Lead me, guides, to where my sisters wait,
   poor sisters of my exile. Let me go
   where I shall never see Cithaeron more,
   where that accursed hill may not see me,°   1385
   where I shall find no trace of thyrsus!
       All that I leave to other Bacchae.

       (*Exit Cadmus and Agave to the side with the bier and attendants.*)

CHORUS [*chanting*]
   The gods have many shapes.°
   The gods bring many things
   to accomplishment unhoped.
   And what was most expected   1390
   has not been accomplished.
   But god has found his way
   for what no man expected.
       So ends this story.

APPENDIX TO THE BACCHAE

This appendix provides Arrowsmith's hypothetical version of the section missing after line 1329.

AGAVE
I am in anguish now,
tormented, who walked in triumph minutes past,
exulting in my kill. And that prize I carried home
with such pride was my own curse. Upon these hands
I bear the curse of my son's blood. How then
with these accursed hands may I touch his body?
How can I, accursed with such a curse, hold him
to my breast? O gods, what dirge can I sing
[that there might be] a dirge [for every]
broken limb?

. . . .

Where is a shroud to cover up his corpse?
O my child, what hands will give you proper care
unless with my own hands I lift my curse?

>   (She lifts up one of Pentheus' limbs and asks the help of
>   Cadmus in piecing the body together. She mourns each
>   piece separately before replacing it on the bier.)

Come, Father. We must restore his head
to this unhappy boy. As best we can, we shall make
him whole again.
—O dearest, dearest face!
Pretty boyish mouth! Now with this veil

I shroud your head, gathering with loving care
these mangled bloody limbs, this flesh I brought
to birth

.   .   .   .

CHORUS LEADER

Let this scene teach those [who see these things:
Dionysus is the son] of Zeus.

(Above the palace Dionysus appears in epiphany.)

DIONYSUS

[I am Dionysus,
the son of Zeus, returned to Thebes, revealed,
a god to men.] But the men [of Thebes] blasphemed me.
They slandered me; they said I came of mortal man,
and not content with speaking blasphemies,
[they dared to threaten my person with violence.]
These crimes this people whom I cherished well
did from malice to their benefactor. Therefore,
I now disclose the sufferings in store for them.
Like [enemies], they shall be driven from this city
to other lands; there, submitting to the yoke
of slavery, they shall wear out wretched lives,
captives of war, enduring much indignity.

(He turns to the corpse of Pentheus.)

This man has found the death which he deserved,
torn to pieces among the jagged rocks.
You are my witnesses: he came with outrage;
he attempted to chain my hands, abusing me
[and doing what he should least of all have done.]
And therefore he has rightly perished by the hands
of those who should the least of all have murdered him.
What he suffers, he suffers justly.

                                        Upon you,
Agave, and on your sisters I pronounce this doom:

you shall leave this city in expiation
of the murder you have done. You are unclean,
and it would be a sacrilege that murderers
should remain at peace beside the graves [of those
whom they have killed].

(He turns to Cadmus.)

IPHIGENIA IN AULIS

Translated by CHARLES R. WALKER

IPHIGENIA IN AULIS: INTRODUCTION

The Play: Date and Composition

Euripides' *Iphigenia in Aulis* was first produced posthumously by his son (also named Euripides) at the Great Dionysian festival in 405 BCE, together with *The Bacchae* (preserved) and *Alcmaeon in Corinth* (lost). Euripides had died the year before while visiting King Archelaus in Macedonia. His trilogy won the first prize; we do not know the names of the other tragedians competing that year, nor the titles of their plays. Presumably Euripides originally entitled this play simply *Iphigenia*, and the further specification was added later, perhaps by the librarians in Alexandria during the Hellenistic period who collected and catalogued the plays by the three great tragedians, in order to distinguish it from his *Iphigenia among the Taurians*.

The play as transmitted presents a number of anomalous features. Its opening scene contains both a spoken explanatory prologue by Agamemnon of the usual Euripidean type and an unparalleled (but very effective) chanted dialogue between him and his aged servant. Then in the course of the play the dramaturgy and certain aspects of the language are frequently incompatible with Euripides' usual style and the conventions of fifth-century BCE tragedy. Finally, toward the end the lengthy messenger's speech recounting Iphigenia's sacrifice and miraculous rescue makes numerous gross metrical errors that cannot be explained away as mistakes in the transmission of the play but seem instead to reflect Byzantine habits of verse composition. In addition, a Greek author of the Roman Imperial period cites as coming from Euripides' *Iphigenia* two and a half lines of a speech by Artemis *ex machina* that are not transmitted in the play as we have it (and that do not necessarily derive from Euripides either); these lines are included in the textual note to the appendix after line 1531.

Almost all scholars are therefore convinced that in the form in which we have it *Iphigenia in Aulis* cannot possibly be a direct, whole product of Euripides alone. Instead, it seems likely that Euripides left the play unfinished at his death and that some of the apparent oddities are due to his son, who staged it in 405 BCE; it also seems likely that at some point much later (perhaps at the very end of antiquity) the pages containing the ending of the play were lost and replaced—or may have been simply rewritten—by someone else. Whether other oddities are the result of further revision, perhaps for a performance sometime during the course of antiquity, is unknown and controversial.

The Myth

Iphigenia in Aulis presents one of the most harrowing episodes in the tragic vicissitudes of the house of the Pelopids, the royal dynasty of Argos (or Mycenae): Agamemnon, his wife Clytemnestra, her lover Aegisthus, and her children Iphigenia, Electra, and Orestes. When the Greek armies under the command of Agamemnon gathered at Aulis in order to sail against Troy, they were held up by adverse winds. The Greek seer Calchas declared that they would be able to sail only if Iphigenia were sacrificed to Artemis; and Agamemnon, after some hesitation, agreed. The maiden was put to death by her father in front of the whole Greek army—though, according to some versions, at the very last moment the goddess miraculously rescued her and substituted a deer. Years later, after the Trojan War had ended, Agamemnon returned home only to be murdered by his wife, whose multiple motives included a strong desire for vengeance for the death of their daughter.

The story of Iphigenia's sacrifice had been narrated in the Homeric *Cypria* (the first component of the epic Trojan Cycle; now lost), and was also mentioned in well-known poems by Hesiod, Stesichorus, Aeschylus, and many others before Euripides came to compose his play. Some of these versions included the detail that Achilles was supposed to marry Iphigenia, thus providing the pretext for summoning her and her mother Clytemnestra to Aulis.

Euripides' play focuses on this single episode, the sacrifice of Iphigenia, dramatizing the events with a distinctive mixture of psychological intensity, pathos, irony, and astonishing reversals. It begins with Agamemnon trying in vain to rescind his request that Clytemnestra bring Iphigenia to the Greek army at Aulis so that Achilles can marry her. (Achilles has no idea that he has been used as a pretext to lure the girl to her death.) Clytemnestra arrives with the girl (and with Orestes, still a baby), and she and Achilles discover the ruse. When the bloodthirsty Greek army finds out about Calchas' oracle and demands that Iphigenia be killed, Achilles is ready to fight to the death in a noble but futile attempt to rescue her—but then the girl freely decides to let herself be sacrificed in order to guarantee the success of the invasion and protect the honor of Greece. The play, as presented in 405 BCE, probably ended at line 1531 with Iphigenia leaving the stage for her death and the chorus acclaiming her decision. In the manuscript, however, this is followed by a second messenger's speech telling of the preparations for the girl's sacrifice and her miraculous rescue by the substitution of a doe slain on the goddess's altar, and then by a very brief closing scene in which Agamemnon returns to announce his departure for Troy.

The episode dramatized in Euripides' *Iphigenia in Aulis* belongs to one of the most popular sets of stories in all of Greek tragedy. In the course of his dramatic career Euripides himself had repeatedly treated other parts of this mythic complex, notably in *Electra* (written ca. 420 BCE), *Iphigenia among the Taurians* (produced ca. 414 BCE), and *Orestes* (produced just three years before, in 408 BCE). Euripides' play also bears an especially close relation to Homer's *Iliad* and Aeschylus' *Oresteia*, for which it is obviously designed as a kind of "prequel": it gives background information relating to preceding events which helps us understand, often ironically, the subsequent legendary episodes recounted by those earlier works. We cannot help but view Euripides' Agamemnon, Clytemnestra, and Achilles in the light of their canonical counterparts as presented by Homer and Aeschylus; and we see in their Euripidean versions the seeds of the disastrous personal confrontations and large-scale catastrophes that will develop just a few years later.

Transmission and Reception

Iphigenia in Aulis seems not to have been one of Euripides' most popular plays during antiquity. While the sacrifice of Iphigenia is referred to frequently in ancient literature and art, it is seldom possible to decide how much this one play or other versions of the story have inspired a later treatment. It survived antiquity only by being among the so-called "alphabetic plays" (see "Introduction to Euripides," p. 3); it is transmitted only by a single manuscript (and its copies), and it is not accompanied by ancient commentaries (scholia) explaining interpretive difficulties. Further evidence that its popularity in antiquity was limited is that only three papyri bearing parts of its text have been discovered.

But in the modern period *Iphigenia in Aulis* has proven to be one of Euripides' most durable successes. It was translated by Erasmus into Latin (1506) and by Lady Jane Lumley into English (1558, apparently the first English translation of Euripides). Important theatrical versions include ones by Jean Rotrou (1640), Jean Racine (1674), Friedrich Schiller (1790), and more recently by Gerhart Hauptmann (1943) and Kenneth Rexroth (1951); Federico García Lorca sketched out a drama on the subject but never finished it (1936).

Starting in the seventeenth century, portrayals of Iphigenia being sacrificed became a popular subject for painters, doubtless because of their mixture of virtue and eroticism: notable examples include a fresco by Domenichino (1609), numerous paintings by Giovanni Battista Tiepolo and his son Giovanni Domenico Tiepolo, and versions by Jan Steen (1671) and Jacques-Louis David (1819). Even Mark Rothko painted a *Sacrifice of Iphi-*

genia in 1942, as did the Belgian surrealist Paul Delvaux in 1968. The story was a favorite one for operas in the eighteenth century—indeed, Diderot recommended it in his "Entretiens sur *Le fils naturel*" (1757) as an ideal subject—and it was set to music by Domenico Scarlatti (1713), Christoph Willibald Gluck (a ballet 1765, an opera 1774), Luigi Cherubini (1782), and many others; as late as 1970 P. D. Q. Bach composed a satirical version, *Iphigenia in Brooklyn*. Other notable twentieth-century versions include the dance by Isadora Duncan to the music of Gluck (1905), the adaptations of some of the choral songs by H.D. (Hilda Doolittle, 1915), a poem by Zbigniew Herbert (1957), a widely distributed film by Michael Cacoyannis starring Irene Papas (1977), and Ariane Mnouchkine's use of this tragedy as the opening play for *Les Atrides*, her adaptation of the *Oresteia* (1990-92).

At the beginning of the twenty-first century, Barry Unsworth wrote a successful novel based upon Euripides' tragedy, *The Songs of the Kings* (2002). The play's continuing vitality on the American stage is demonstrated not only by increasingly frequent performances of translations but also by such recent productions as Neil LaBute's short play *Iphigenia in Orem* (2000), Caridad Svich's multimedia play *Iphigenia Crash Land Falls on the Neon Shell That Was Once Her Heart (a rave fable)* (2004), and Charles L. Mee's *Iphigenia 2.0* (2007). As long as audiences continue to be fascinated by the violence of men against women, the bloodthirstiness of war, and the conflict between moral nobility and sordid utilitarianism, *Iphigenia in Aulis* will surely remain popular.

IPHIGENIA IN AULIS

Characters   AGAMEMNON, commander-in-chief of the
Greek army
OLD MAN, servant of Agamemnon
CHORUS of women from Chalcis
MENELAUS, brother of Agamemnon
MESSENGER
CLYTEMNESTRA, wife of Agamemnon
IPHIGENIA, daughter of Agamemnon and
Clytemnestra
ORESTES (nonspeaking character)
ACHILLES, the greatest Greek warrior
SECOND MESSENGER

*Scene: In front of the tent of Agamemnon in the camp of the Greek
army at Aulis.*

(Enter Agamemnon from his tent, carrying a letter.)

AGAMEMNON [*chanting throughout this opening scene*]
  Old man, come out in front of the tent.

OLD MAN [*also chanting throughout this scene, at first from within*]
  I'm coming!
  What strange new plan have you got in your head,
  my lord Agamemnon?

AGAMEMNON
  Hurry up!

(Enter Old Man from the tent.)

OLD MAN

I'm hurrying—and I'm not asleep.
Sleep rests light on these old eyes.
I can look sharp.   5

AGAMEMNON

Well, what is that malignant star
that moves high across the sky
next to the seven Pleiades?°
No voice is there of birds even,
or of the seas' waves.
The silence of the winds   10
holds hushed the Euripus strait.

OLD MAN

Yes, but why have you been rushing
up and down, my lord Agamemnon,
outside your tent? There's peace
and quiet here at Aulis
and the guards are quiet too
over on the walls of the fort.
They don't move at all. Can we   15
not go inside now?

AGAMEMNON

    I envy you, old man,
I am jealous of men who without peril
pass through their lives, obscure,
unknown; least of all do I envy
those vested with honors.

Responsibility

OLD MAN

Oh, but these have a glory in their lives!   20

AGAMEMNON

Ah—a glory that is perilous.
High honors are sweet, but ever

Perilous glory

[94] EURIPIDES

they stand close to the brink of grief.
At one time, the gods
overturn a man's life. At another,   25
the wills of men, many and malignant,
ruin life utterly.

OLD MAN
                    I don't like words
like these from a king. Agamemnon,
Atreus begat you, but not to have
all good things in your life. No,   30
it is necessary that you be glad
and sad too, for you were born
mortal, and whether you like it or not,
that's what the gods wish.
But you've lit your lamp and
been writing a letter: 35
you still have it in your hand.
You write words—and then
you erase them. You seal
the letter up—and then tear
the seal open. Then you
throw the writing tablet on the ground,
and bulging tears come down out   40
of your eyes. My lord, you act
helpless, and mad! What is the pain,
what is the new thing of agony,
O my king? Tell it to me, for I
am a good man and a loyal servant;
so you can speak. I was given   45
to your wife, part of the wedding dowry,
and Tyndareus picked me for this service
because I was honest.

AGAMEMNON [*now speaking*]
    To Leda, Thestius' daughter, were born three girls:
    Phoebe; Clytemnestra, whom I married;   50

and Helen. To seek her hand, the finest youths
of Greece came wooing. But each one threatened murder
against the others, if he were unsuccessful.
Her father Tyndareus had a problem: 55
whether he should let her marry one or not,
how best escape disaster at fate's hands.
Then he had this idea: he'd bind the suitors
by oath and handshake, seal it by sacrifice,   60
that whoever won Helen, the others would defend him.
And if any man should steal her from his house,
then all must go to war against that man
and sack his town, be it barbarian or Greek.   65
The shrewd old man persuaded them. And once
they'd sworn, he let his daughter choose whichever
suitor love's honeyed breezes might carry her to.
She chose Menelaus—if only she had not!   70
For to Sparta came from Phrygia the man who judged
the goddesses—at least, so runs men's story.
He came with flowery clothing and bright gold,
barbarian opulence. So Helen loved him,
and he loved her. Her husband was away,   75
so he carried her off to the pasturelands of Ida.
But Menelaus, furious with desire,
invoked throughout all Greece Tyndareus' oath,
that the suitors must now help him in his plight.

So all the Greeks sprang to their arms, and now   80
they've all come here to the narrow straits of Aulis
with many ships and shields and horses and chariots.
And since I am the brother of Menelaus,   85
to please him they chose me as their commander.
If only someone else had won that honor!
For once the army was mustered here at Aulis,
a dead calm kept us sitting. We were baffled.
And then the seer Calchas prophesied:
Iphigenia, my own daughter, must be slaughtered   90

for Artemis, the goddess of this place.
If she were sacrificed then we would sail
and overthrow the Phrygians; otherwise
this would not be. When I heard this, I told
Talthybius, our herald, to proclaim
that I dismissed the army—I would never   95
be cruel enough to murder my own daughter!
But then my brother argued and convinced me
to commit this horror. So I wrote a letter,
I sealed it and I sent it to my wife,
telling her to send our daughter here
to marry Achilles. I praised his reputation   100
and said he would not sail unless a bride
came from our family to his home in Phthia.
This lie about her marriage I contrived
to persuade my wife. The only Greeks who know   105
are Calchas, and Odysseus, and Menelaus.

     I did this wrong! Now I'm setting things right
by writing this new letter which you saw
me sealing and unsealing in the dark.   110
But take this letter now, and quick, to Argos!
The message folded here, all that is written,
I'll tell you now myself, since you are loyal,
faithful both to my wife and to my house.

OLD MAN [*chanting throughout this interchange with Agamemnon,*
who chants in response]
  Tell me then and show me—so that°   115
  the words I speak with my tongue
  will say the same as the letter.

AGAMEMNON
  "Child of Leda, Clytemnestra:
  this letter will bring you
  a new message. Do not send your daughter
  to the calm beach of Aulis, here   120

in the harbor facing Euboea.
Let us wait another season before
we celebrate our child's marriage."

OLD MAN

But when Achilles loses his bride—
won't his heart blow up in fierce   125
anger against you and against
your wife? Oh, this is
a dangerous thing! Tell me
what you say.

AGAMEMNON

                    I'll tell you—
not in fact but in name only
is there a marriage with Achilles.
He knows nothing of it or of our plan
or that I have said I would give him   130
my daughter as his bride.

OLD MAN

To bring her here a victim then—
a death offering—though you promised   135
her to the son of the goddess!
Oh, you have dared a dreadful deed,
my lord Agamemnon!

AGAMEMNON

My mind was crazed, I fell into madness!
No—you must get on your way and run.
Forget that your legs are old.

OLD MAN

I will hurry, my lord.   140

AGAMEMNON

Don't rest by the forest springs
or give in to sleep.

OLD MAN

    No, no!

AGAMEMNON

  When you come to any fork in the road
  look keenly both ways and be sure   145
  their carriage doesn't pass quickly—
  when you are not looking—and so
  bring my daughter right to
  the Greek ships.

OLD MAN

    I will!

AGAMEMNON

        And if you
  meet her and her escort,°
  turn them back! Yes, take the reins   150
  and shake them, send them back
  to Argos, back to the city built by the Cyclopes.

OLD MAN

  Wait. When I say these things,
  tell me, what will make your wife
  and your daughter trust me?   155

AGAMEMNON

  This seal on the letter
  you're carrying—do not break it!
  Now go! The dawn is here, and
  the sun's chariot already is
  making the day bright. Go do this task!   160
  No mortal man has happiness
  and fortune in all ways. He is
  born, every man, to his grief!

Every man to his grief

        (*Exit Old Man to the side, Agamemnon into*
            his tent. Enter Chorus from the side.)

CHORUS [*singing*]

I have come to the shore
and the sea sands of Aulis   165
over Euripus' waters
and the sea narrows, sailing
from Chalcis, my city,
Chalcis, nurse to the fountain
Arethusa, sea-surrounded   170
and famous—to see this host
of noble Achaeans, with their oar-borne ships
of heroes, whom Menelaus, the yellow-haired,   175
and Agamemnon, nobly born—our husbands tell us—
sent in a thousand galleys
to seek out Helen and seize her;
Helen, whom Paris the herdsman   180
took from the banks of the river,
reedy Eurotas—Aphrodite bestowed her—
on the day when the Cyprian held—
near a dewy spring—
a battle of beauty
with Hera and Pallas Athena.

Through the sacrificial grove,   185
Artemis' grove, I came swift running;
in my eagerness, my cheeks
blushing with young modesty—in my yearning to see
the Danaans' wall of shields,
the war gear by each tent,   190
and the great host of their horses.
And now those two whose names are Ajax
I looked upon, sitting together,
the son of Oileus, and Telamon's child
who is the crown and pride

of Salamis. And playing at draughts,
delighting in its trickery,
was Protesilaus,   195
with him Palamedes the sea god's son.
Another hurled the discus, Diomedes,   200
and took great joy in it.
And next to Meriones, Ares' kin,
at whom all mortals marvel,
was Laertes' son from his mountainous island
and Nireus, handsomest seeming
of all the Achaeans.   205

Swift-footed Achilles I saw—
his feet like the stormwind—running,
Achilles whom Thetis bore, and
Chiron trained into manhood.
I saw him on the seashore,   210
in full armor over the sands racing.
He strove, his legs in contest
with a chariot and four,
toward victory racing and rounding
the course. And Eumelus, Pheres' grandson,
the charioteer, cried forth in frenzy.   215
I saw his handsome horses there,
gold-wrought in bits and harness.
Eumelus with his goad struck them,   220
the yoke horses' manes dappled gray,
and the trace horses that flanked them
and grazed the post at the end of the race course—   225
they were fiery-haired, with their fetlocks
spotted. And always beside them Peleus' son
hurled himself onward in his armor,
right by the chariot's car rail,
right by the spinning axle.   230

And then I came upon the fleet,
an indescribable wonder, so that
with joy my woman's eyes were filled.
The armament of Myrmidons from Phthia
were there on the right, swift ships, fifty of them.   235
Upon their sterns set high in gold,
the divine daughters of the sea lord Nereus   240
carved as symbols of Achilles' host.

Keel by keel beside them
lay as many Argive ships
commanded by Mecisteus' son—
his grandfather Talaus fostered him to manhood   245
and Sthenelus, Capaneus' son.
And leader of the Attic ships in number sixty,
the son of Theseus, who had anchored them
in an even line, and with insignia,
Pallas Athena in her chariot   250
drawn by winged horses,
a clear sign to his mariners.

In Boeotia's naval squadron
I counted fifty ships
fitted with blazonry;   255
Cadmus on each of them
with his golden dragon
high on their sterns lifted.
It was Leitus the earth-born
who commanded the squadron.   260
Next from the land of Phocis . . .°
. . . captain of Locrian ships
of equal number was the son of Oileus,
who had embarked from Thronium,   265
illustrious city.

From Mycenae, walled by the Cyclopes,
the son of Atreus brought his ships,
a hundred galleys in order;
with him his brother,
commander and kinsman,
sailing to wreak revenge on her
who had fled his hearth   270
to accomplish a barbarian marriage.
From Pylos, Gerenian Nestor's
ships I beheld;°
... on their sterns emblazoned
bull-bodied Alpheus,   275
Alpheus, the river that runs by his home.

EPODE

Twelve Aenianian ships were there
with Gouneus the king as captain.
Hard by, the lords of Elis   280
whom they all called Epeians;
their ships Eurytus led,
and the Taphian squadron—
oars gleaming white in the sunlight—
was led by Meges,° Phyleus' son.   285
He had set sail from the Echinae isles,
a rocky terror to mariners.
Ajax, Salamis born,
linked the right wing of the navy to the left,°   290
knitting together the nearest and farthest
galleys. And for that linkage
he moved his own twelve ships, easy to pilot.
So I heard, and saw his crew.   295
No home-going will there be
for any barbarian craft
which grapples with these—
such a navy setting forth   300

I've seen on this day,
and what I heard at home and remember,
the marshaled army.

(*Enter Menelaus and the Old Man from the side.*)

OLD MAN

Menelaus! You have dared a fearful thing
that goes against all conscience.

MENELAUS

Stand back!
You're a slave—too loyal to your master!

OLD MAN

The reproach you've given me—it is an honor. 305

MENELAUS

Keep your place—or you'll pay for it in pain.

OLD MAN

You had no right to open the letter I carried!

MENELAUS

Nor had you the right to carry a message
that brings evil and disaster to all Greece.

OLD MAN

I'll argue that with others—give me the letter.

MENELAUS

I will not give it. 310

OLD MAN

And I won't let it go!

MENELAUS

This scepter will beat your head into a bloody pulp.

OLD MAN

To die for my lord would be a glorious death.

MENELAUS

Hands off—you talk too much for a slave.

OLD MAN   *(Shouting toward the tent.)*

O my king, look how we're being wronged!
He took your letter—tore it from my hand   315
by force. And now, he won't listen to right
or to reason.°

(Enter Agamemnon from his tent.)

AGAMEMNON

What is this—a brawl
and argument right at my own door?

MENELAUS

More than this man I have the right to speak.

AGAMEMNON

What brought you into dispute with him, and why
such violence?

(The Old Man goes out.)

MENELAUS

Look at me, Agamemnon;   320
then I will begin to speak my piece.

AGAMEMNON

I am the son of Atreus. Do you think
I shrink from your eye, Menelaus?

MENELAUS

Do you see this tablet, bearer of shameful writing?

AGAMEMNON

I see the letter. First, give it to me.

MENELAUS

Not till I've shown its message to all the Greeks.

AGAMEMNON

So now you know what you have no right   325
to know. You broke the seal!

MENELAUS

Yes, I broke it
and to your sorrow. You'll suffer now
for the evil you secretly plotted!

AGAMEMNON

Where did you find it? Oh, you have no shame!

MENELAUS

I was watching to see if your daughter
had arrived at the camp out of Argos.

AGAMEMNON

It's true—you have no shame. What reason
have you for spying on my affairs?

MENELAUS

My own desire
urged me. I am not one of your slaves.   330

AGAMEMNON

Can there be any outrage like this?
You won't allow me to rule in my own house!

MENELAUS

No, for your mind is shifty: yesterday
one thing, today another, another tomorrow.

AGAMEMNON

You frame
wickedness neatly. Oh, I hate a smooth tongue!

MENELAUS

Agamemnon,
a disloyal heart is false to friends and
a thing of evil. Now I want to question you;   335
so don't, because you are angry, turn your face

from the truth—I shall not rack you too hard.
    Have you forgotten when you were eager
and anxious to lead the Greek army to Troy,
wanting to appear unambitious but in your heart
eager for command? Do you remember how humble
you were to all the people, grasping the hand,
keeping open the doors of your house, yes,   340
open to all, granting to every man, even the lowly,
the right to address and to hail you by name?
These ways and tricks you tried, to buy
in the market advancement, but when at last
you won power, then you turned these habits
of your heart inside out. Now were you
no longer loving to your friends of yesterday.
Unapproachable, you were seldom found at home.   345
When a good man has won to the heights of power,
he shouldn't put on new manners for old and change
his countenance. Far more when he's in fortune
and able truly to succor, must he hold
firmly to old friends.
                This is my first point
against you. First I blame you for these things
where I have found you ignoble. Then when
you came to Aulis with the army—   350
from being all, you became nothing,
confounded by a fate god-given, lacking
a favoring wind. So the Danaans urged
that you send back all the ships and at Aulis
put an end to this toil without meaning.
I remember your face then, bewildered,
unhappy, fearing you would never captain
your thousand ships or fill up with spears   355
the fields of Priam's Troy. Then you called me
into council. "What shall I do?" you asked me.
"What scheme, what strategy can I devise
that will prevent the stripping-off

of my command and the loss of my glorious name?"
  Calchas spoke: "Sacrifice on the altar
your own daughter to Artemis, and the Greek ships
will sail." At that instant your heart filled up
with gladness and happily, in sacrifice,   360
you promised to slay the child. So you
sent willingly to your wife, not by compulsion—
you cannot deny that—that she send the girl
here, and for pretext, that she come to marry
Achilles. And yet now you have been caught
changing your mind; in secret you recast
the message. So now your story?—you will
never be your daughter's murderer! This is
the very same heaven which heard you say these words.   365
  Thousands have done what you have done—willingly
struggled and striven, and then they fail
and fall in ignominy. Now in some instances
the populace is responsible out of stupidity,
but with other men the failure is their own
as they can't protect their city. Oh, how I groan
now on behalf of Greece in her affliction;   370
for she was ready to perform a noble deed,
but on account of your daughter and you,
she's letting those worthless barbarians slip away
and mock her name! O may I never make
any man ruler of my country or
commander of her armies just because
of his bravery. No, a good commander
must have sense. Any smart man will do.   375

CHORUS LEADER
  Terrible are these fighting words that lead
  brothers into strife with one another.

AGAMEMNON
  Now will I give you briefly my reproach.
  Nor will my looks grow haughty with contempt,

but looking and speaking I'll be temperate,
as it befits a brother, and as a good man   380
to another shows decency and respect.
You're breathing hard and red-faced—why? Tell me,
who wrongs you, what do you want? Are you
burning to possess a virtuous wife? Well,
I can't procure her for you. The one you had
you governed poorly. Should I pay the price
for your mistakes, when I am innocent?
It is not my advancement that bites your heart.   385
No, you've thrown to the winds all reason
and honor, and lust only to hold a lovely woman
in your arms. Oh, the pleasures of the base
are always vile. And now—if yesterday
I was without wit or wisdom, but today
I've counseled with myself well and wisely—
does that make me mad? Rather are you crazed,
for the gods, being generous, rid you of
a wicked wife, yet now you want her back!   390
As to the suitors, marriage-mad, with folly
in their hearts, they swore an oath to Tyndareus.
Yes, I grant that; but Hope is a god, and she,
not any power of yours, put it into effect.
Make war with their help—they'll join you in their folly!
But in heaven there is intelligence—it can°
perceive oaths bonded in evil, under compulsion   395
sworn. So I will not kill my children!
Nor will your enterprise of vengeance upon
an evil wife prosper against all justice.
If I were to commit this act, against law, right,
and the child I fathered, each day, each night,
while I yet lived would wear me out in grief
and tears.
       So these are my few words, clear   400
and easily understood. You may choose madness,
but I will order my affairs in decency and honor.

CHORUS LEADER

How different are these words from those you spoke
before! How good it is to save one's children.

MENELAUS

O gods—so now I have no friends. Poor me!

AGAMEMNON

You do, but not if you're wishing to destroy them.   405

MENELAUS

How will you prove you are our father's son,
my brother?

AGAMEMNON

                              I am brother to you
when you are sane, not mad.

MENELAUS

                              Should not
a friend share with friends his grief?

AGAMEMNON

Speak when you have befriended me,
not done me injury.

MENELAUS

                              Isn't it right that you   410
should bear a part of Greece's hardship?

AGAMEMNON

This is what I think—Greece, like yourself,
some god has driven mad.

MENELAUS

                              You have a king's
scepter—boast of it and puff yourself up!
To me you are a traitor, so I'll turn
to other means and other friends.

                              (Enter Messenger from the side.)

MESSENGER

    O commander of all the armies of Greece,
    King Agamemnon, I have come to bring   415
    to you your daughter, Iphigenia,
    and her mother who is with her,
    the queen, Clytemnestra.
    And the boy Orestes is here—you've been
    so long from home that, seeing him, delight
    will fill your heart.
          Now after weary travel, beside a fountain   420
    free flowing, the ladies rest and bathe
    their feet. So do the horses—on the green
    meadow we've turned them loose to browse.
          I have come, running ahead of the others
    to prepare you with this information:
    rumor travels fast and by now the army   425
    knows that your daughter has arrived in Aulis.
    In fact, crowds from the camp already have come
    on the run for a sight of the maiden.
    For the fortunate are glorious and all men
    gaze at them. Now they are saying: "Is it
    a marriage, or what happens now?   430
    Has King Agamemnon so yearned in love
    for his daughter that now he has brought her
    to Aulis?" This too you could hear them say:
  "They're making the marriage offering to Artemis,
    Aulis' queen, but who will be the bridegroom?"
          So let's prepare barley for sacrifice,   435
    let us crown our heads with garlands, and you,
    King Menelaus, start the bridal hymn!
    Oh, let the pipes be played, and there should be
    dancing within the pavilion, since for
    the maid this day should dawn in happiness.

AGAMEMNON

    You are thanked for your news. Now you may go   440

inside the pavilion. As to the rest—
it will go well, as the fates will it.

(Exit the Messenger into the tent.)

O god, how can I find words or begin
to speak in the face of this, my disaster?
I've fallen under the yoke of fate.
I forged a clever scheme, but cleverer far   445
was a deity. O fortunate men of mean,
ignoble birth, freely you may weep and
empty out your hearts, but the highborn—
we suffer, decorum rules our lives and we,
by service to the mob, become its slaves.   450

     I am ashamed of these tears. And yet
at this extremity of my misfortune
I am ashamed not to shed them. What words
can I utter to my wife or with what countenance
receive and welcome her? Her appearance here,   455
unsummoned, means disaster for me now.
Yet coming she only obeys nature,
following a daughter here to do love's service,
and give the bride away. So doing, she
shall find me out as the author of this evil.

     And the unhappy maiden! Maiden, no—   460
soon, it seems, Hades will marry her.
Oh, piteous fate! I hear her cry to me:
"O Father, why do you kill me? May you too
have such a marriage, and all your friends as well!"
Beside her, Orestes the infant will cry out   465
meaningless words, but full of meaning
to my heart!

     O Paris, it is your marriage to Helen
that has wrought these things and my destruction!

CHORUS LEADER
And I too grieve, so far as a stranger may,
over a king's misfortune.   470

MENELAUS

My brother, grant me this, to grasp your hand.

AGAMEMNON

Here it is. You have won the mastery.
I now face the ordeal of my defeat.

MENELAUS

No! I swear by Pelops, father of our
father, and by Atreus, who begot us both,
that truly now I do not speak toward   475
any end but inwardly and from my heart.
When I saw tears bursting from your eyes
tears started in mine and a great pity
seized me. I am no longer terrible   480
to you, or any more your enemy.
I retract my words. I stand now in your place
and beseech you, do not slay your child
and do not prefer my interests to your own.
It is against all justice that you should
groan while my life is happy—that your children
should die while mine look on the bright sun's light.
         What do I want? Could I not obtain   485
a perfect marriage elsewhere, if I longed for
marrying? But a brother, whom I should
most cherish, I was about to forfeit
to gain a Helen, so bartering excellence
for evil. I was witless and adolescent
until, crowding upon the deed, I saw and knew
all that it meant to kill a child.   490
Besides this, thinking upon our kinship,
pity for the girl in her harsh agony
swept over me: she would be killed
on account of my marriage. But what has Helen
to do with this girl of yours? Disband
the host, I say, let it go from Aulis,   495
and so cease drowning your eyes in tears

and summoning me to grieve and weep for you.
As to your share in the dire oracle
concerning your daughter's destiny, I
want no part in it; my share I give to you.
And so I've turned my threatening words   500
into their opposites? But it is fitting;
I have changed because I love a brother.
A good man always tries to act for the best.

CHORUS LEADER
O King, you honor your forefathers—   505
a speech worthy of Tantalus, Zeus' son.

AGAMEMNON
I thank you, Menelaus, that now
beyond my hopes you have spoken justly,
with right reason, worthy of yourself.
These quarrels between brothers spring from
many things, over a woman, for instance,
or out of greed for an inheritance.
I loathe the kind of kinship that pours pain   510
into both hearts. But we have arrived
at a fatal place: a compulsion absolute
forces the slaughter of my child.

MENELAUS
What do you mean? Who will force you to kill her?

AGAMEMNON
The whole concourse of the Achaean army.

MENELAUS
No—not if you send her back to Argos.   515

AGAMEMNON
I might do that secretly—but from the army
there's something else I could not keep secret.

MENELAUS
What? You're wrong to fear the mob so desperately.

AGAMEMNON

 Listen to me. To the whole Greek army
 Calchas will report the prophecy.

MENELAUS

 Not if he dies first—that's an easy matter.

AGAMEMNON

 The whole race of prophets is an ambitious evil.   520

MENELAUS

 They're useless when you really need their help;°
 and when they're useful, all they cause is pain.

AGAMEMNON

 Menelaus, do you feel none of the terror
 which creeps into my heart?

MENELAUS

      How can I know
 Your fear if you do not name it?

AGAMEMNON

         Odysseus,
 son of Sisyphus, knows all these things.

MENELAUS

 Odysseus is not the man to cause us pain.   525

AGAMEMNON

 He's cunning and he always backs the mob.

MENELAUS

 Ambition rules his soul—a dreadful evil!

AGAMEMNON

 So won't he stand amongst the soldiers and
 tell the prophecy which Calchas spoke
 and how I promised to sacrifice   530
 a victim to Artemis—and how I then
 annulled my promises? Oh, with these words

won't he arouse and seize the very soul
of the army, order them to kill you
and me—and sacrifice the girl?

If I should escape to Argos they then
would follow me there, and even to
the Cyclopean walls to raze them
to the earth and utterly destroy the land.   535
Such is the terrible circumstance in which
I find myself. Now in my despair I am
quite helpless, and it is the gods' will.
Do this one thing for me, Menelaus,
go through the army, take all precaution
that Clytemnestra learn nothing of this
till after I have seized my child and   540
sent her to her death. So I may do
this evil thing with fewest tears.
You foreign ladies, see that you guard your lips.

(Exit Agamemnon into the tent, and Menelaus to the side.)

CHORUS [singing]

STROPHE

O blest are those who share
in Aphrodite's gifts   545
with modesty and measure,
blest who escape the frenzied passion.
For Eros of the golden hair
shoots two arrows of desire,
and the one brings happiness   550
to man's life, the other ruin.
O Cypris, loveliest of goddesses
in heaven, keep the frenzied arrow
from my bedroom.
Keep modest my delights,
all my desires lawful,   555
so may I have my part in love
but not in passion's madness.

Various are the natures
of mortals, diverse their ways,
yet a straight path is always the right one;   560
and lessons deeply taught
lead man to paths of righteousness;
restraint, I say, is wisdom
and by its grace we see virtue°
with a right judgment.   565
From all of this springs honor
bringing ageless glory into
man's life. Oh, a mighty quest
is the hunting out of virtue—
which for womankind
must be a love kept hidden,
but, for men, if good order is fully there,°   570
it augments the state.

EPODE

O Paris, you returned to°
the land which reared you,
herdsman of white heifers
upon Ida's mountains; where   575
barbarian melodies you played
upon a shepherd's reeds
and echoed there once more
Olympus' Phrygian pipe.
Full-uddered cattle browsed
when the goddesses summoned you   580
for their trial of beauty—
the trial that sent you
to Greece, to stand before
an ivory throne; it was there
looking into Helen's eyes
you gave and took the ecstasies of love.   585
So from this quarrel comes

the assault by Greeks
with ship and spear
upon Troy's citadel.°

(Enter Clytemnestra, Iphigenia, and baby
Orestes from the side in a carriage.)

CHORUS [now chanting]
Hail, hail!°   590
The good fortune of the mighty
is mighty! Behold
Iphigenia, the king's daughter,
my queen, and Clytemnestra,
daughter of Tyndareus.
They, sprung from the mighty ones,
ride on to highest destiny.   595
The gods themselves, bestowers of happiness,
seem not more august
than these
to the less fortunate amongst mankind.

Now let us stand here, children of Chalcis,
let us receive the queen
out of her chariot
and keep her step from stumbling   600
to the earth.
Gently, with good will,
with our hands
we will help you down.
O noble daughter of Agamemnon,
newly come to Aulis, have no fear!
For to you, stranger from Argos—   605
gently and without clamor
we who are strangers too
let us give you our welcome.

CLYTEMNESTRA [speaking]
I shall think of this as a good omen—

your kindness and good words—for I am here,
hopefully, to lead this young girl   610
into a noble and a happy marriage.
Now, will you take the dowry from the wagon—
all of her bridal gifts which I have brought.
Carry them into the pavilion carefully.
And you, daughter, set down your pretty feet
from the carriage onto the ground. All of you
maidens take her into your arms and help   615
her down.
             And now, will someone lend me
the support of an arm, that with greater
dignity I may dismount—stand in front
of the horses' yoke—see, the colt's eyes are   620
wild with terror!
             Now, this is Agamemnon's son.
Take him—his name is Orestes—he's
still quite a helpless baby.

                              (The Chorus does as instructed.)

                    My baby,
are you still asleep from the rolling wheels?
Wake up and be happy. This is your sister's
wedding day! You are noble, and so
you will have a nobleman as kin,   625
the godlike child of the Nereid.
My child, Iphigenia, come stand next to
your mother. Stay close beside me and show
all these strangers here how happy and how
blessed I am in you! But here he comes—
your most beloved father. Give him welcome.   630

                         (Enter Agamemnon from his tent.)

IPHIGENIA

O Mother, don't be angry if I run
ahead and throw myself into his arms.

CLYTEMNESTRA

Mightiest and most honored, Lord Agamemnon,°
obedient to your command, we are here.

IPHIGENIA

Father!
I long to throw myself before anyone   635
into your arms—it's been so long a time—
and see your face! Oh, are you angry, Mother?

CLYTEMNESTRA

No my child, this is rightful, and it is
as it has always been. Of all the children
I have borne your father, you love him most.

IPHIGENIA

Father, what a desperate age since I   640
saw you last! But now, seeing you again,
I am happy.

AGAMEMNON

                    And I, seeing you,
am happy. You speak for both of us, Iphigenia.

IPHIGENIA

Hail! O Father, it is a good and
wonderful thing you have done—bringing me here!

AGAMEMNON

I do not know how to answer what you say,
my child.

IPHIGENIA

                    Oh? Before you were glad to see me,
but now your eyes have no quiet in them.

AGAMEMNON

I have cares—the many cares of a general   645
and a king.

IPHIGENIA

Oh, turn away from all of them,
my father—be here and mine only, now!

AGAMEMNON

I am. Now I am nowhere but in this place,
and with you utterly, my darling.

IPHIGENIA

Oh then,
unknit your brow, and smooth your face for love.

AGAMEMNON

Now see, my joy at seeing you—what joy it is.

IPHIGENIA

But tears—a libation of tears—are there   650
ready to pour from your eyes.

AGAMEMNON

Well,
there is a long parting about to come
for both of us.

IPHIGENIA

I don't understand,
dear Father, I don't understand.°

AGAMEMNON

And yet
you do seem to speak with understanding,
and I am the more grieved.

IPHIGENIA

I'll speak foolishly
if that will please you more.

AGAMEMNON   *(To himself.)*
How hard to curb my tongue!   655

(To Iphigenia.)

Yes, do.

IPHIGENIA

Now for a time, Father dear, won't you stay
at home with your children?

AGAMEMNON

O that I might!
I want to and I can't—it cracks my heart.

IPHIGENIA

Menelaus' wrongs and his spearmen—O
that they'd disappear!

AGAMEMNON

He and his wrongs
will destroy others first—they've ruined me.

IPHIGENIA

Father, you've been so long in Aulis' gulf!   660

AGAMEMNON

I must
dispatch the armies, but there's something still
hindering me.

IPHIGENIA

Where is it they say°
these Phrygians live, my father?

AGAMEMNON

In the country
where Paris, the son of Priam, dwells, and
would to heaven he had never lived at all!

IPHIGENIA

You're going on a long voyage, leaving me!

AGAMEMNON

But your situation is like mine, my daughter.   665

IPHIGENIA

Oh—on this voyage of yours I only wish°
it were right for you to take me with you!

AGAMEMNON

    It is ordained that you too take a long
    sailing, my daughter, to a land where—where
    you must remember me!°

IPHIGENIA

                Shall I go
    on this voyage with my mother, or alone?

AGAMEMNON

    Alone—cut off and quite separated
    from both your father and your mother.

IPHIGENIA

    A new home you make for me, Father,   670
    do you mean this?

AGAMEMNON

               Now stop—it's not right
    for a girl to know any of these things.

IPHIGENIA

    Father, over there when you have done
    all things well, hurry back to me from Troy!

AGAMEMNON

    I will, but first, right here, in Aulis
    I must offer a sacrifice.

IPHIGENIA

             What kind of rites,
    to try to find what piety requires?

AGAMEMNON

    You shall see this one, for you are to stand   675
    by the basin of holy water.

IPHIGENIA

    Then round the altar shall we start the dance?

AGAMEMNON

O for this happy ignorance that is yours!
Now go into the pavilion—to be seen
embarrasses maidens. But first give me
a kiss and your right hand, for soon you go
to live apart from your father for too long.   680
O breast and cheeks! O golden hair!
What bitter burden Helen and her Troy city
have laid upon us!° I must stop, for as I
touch you my eyes are water springs—the tears
start their escape. Go into the pavilion!   685

                         (*Exit Iphigenia into the tent.*)

Oh, forgive me, child of Leda, for this
self-pity! Here am I giving in marriage
my daughter to Achilles! Such partings
bring happiness but prick the heart of a father
who, after all his fostering care, must give
away a daughter to another's home.   690

CLYTEMNESTRA

I am not unfeeling, nor do I reproach
your grief. For I, too, shall sorrow
as I lead her and as the marriage hymn is sung.
But time and custom will soften sadness.
His name to whom you have betrothed   695
our child I know. Now tell me
his home and lineage.

AGAMEMNON

Asopus had a daughter, Aegina.

CLYTEMNESTRA

Yes. Who married her, god or a mortal?

AGAMEMNON

Zeus married her. Aeacus was their son,
and he became Oenone's ruler.

CLYTEMNESTRA
             Tell me,
which child of Aeacus received the inheritance?   700

AGAMEMNON
    Peleus—he married Nereus' daughter.

CLYTEMNESTRA
    Did the gods bless their marriage
    or did he take her against their will?

AGAMEMNON
    Zeus betrothed her; he approved
    and gave her away in marriage.

CLYTEMNESTRA
             Tell me—where
    did Peleus marry her? Under the sea's waves?

AGAMEMNON
    No, on the holy foothills of Pelion,   705
    where Chiron lives.

CLYTEMNESTRA
             Where they say the tribes
    of Centaurs make their home?

AGAMEMNON
             Yes, and it was there
    the gods gave Peleus a marriage feast.

CLYTEMNESTRA
    Will you tell me this—did Thetis rear
    Achilles or his father?

AGAMEMNON
             Chiron taught him,
    that he might never learn the customs of
    evil men.

CLYTEMNESTRA

         I would say a wise teacher, but
Peleus giving him that teacher was wiser still.   710

AGAMEMNON

So, such a man is your daughter's husband.

CLYTEMNESTRA

A perfect choice! Where is his city in Greece?

AGAMEMNON

It is within Phthia, and beside
the river Apidanus.

CLYTEMNESTRA

         And it's there
that you will bring your child and mine?   715

AGAMEMNON

That should be her husband's care.

CLYTEMNESTRA

Well, I ask heaven's blessings upon them!
What is the day set for the marriage?

AGAMEMNON

When the full moon comes, to bring them good luck.

CLYTEMNESTRA

Now I ask this, have you slain the victims
to Artemis, the goddess, for our child?

AGAMEMNON

I'm about to; I have made all preparations.

CLYTEMNESTRA

And later you will hold the marriage feast?   720

AGAMEMNON

When I've sacrificed to the gods their due.

CLYTEMNESTRA

And where do I make the women's feast?

AGAMEMNON

Here, by these proud sterns of our ships.

CLYTEMNESTRA

That's sordid and unworthy! Well,
may good fortune come of it!

AGAMEMNON

                              My lady,
This you must do—obey!   725

CLYTEMNESTRA

                    That is no revelation—
I am accustomed to it.

AGAMEMNON

                              So here
where the bridegroom is I will . . .

CLYTEMNESTRA

                              Do what?
You'll take what office that is mine as mother?

AGAMEMNON

. . . give the child away—among the sons of Danaus.

CLYTEMNESTRA

And meantime, where must I be staying?   730

AGAMEMNON

Return to Argos, where you must take care
of our younger daughters.

CLYTEMNESTRA

                    Leaving my child?
Who then will lift the marriage torch?

AGAMEMNON

Whatever torch is fitting, I will raise it.

CLYTEMNESTRA

Against all custom! And you see
nothing wrong in that?

AGAMEMNON

       I see that it is
wrong for you to stay, mingling with the host   735
of the army.

CLYTEMNESTRA

       I think it right
a mother give away her daughter.

AGAMEMNON

But wrong, I tell you, to leave the maidens
alone in our halls.

CLYTEMNESTRA

       In maiden chambers
they are safe and well guarded.

AGAMEMNON

                Obey me!

CLYTEMNESTRA

No, by the Argives' goddess queen!
You go outside and do your part, I indoors   740
will do what's proper for the maid's marrying.

                (Exit Clytemnestra into the tent.)

AGAMEMNON

Oh, I have rushed madly into this and failed
in every hope, desiring to send my wife
out of my sight—I a conspirator
against my best beloved and weaving plots
against them. Now I am confounded   745
in all things. Yet to the priest Calchas
I will go, with him to do the goddess' pleasure
though that should spell my doom,
and for Greece toil and travail.
A wise man keeps his wife at home
virtuous and helpful—or never marries.   750

(Exit Agamemnon to the side.)

CHORUS [*singing*]

STROPHE

Now will they come to Simois
and the silvery swirl of her waters—
the Greeks mighty in assembly
with their ships and their armor;
to Ilium, to the plains of Troy   755
sacred to Phoebus Apollo,
where Cassandra is prophet, I hear,
crowned with the green laurel—
and wildly she flings her golden hair
as the god breathes into her soul   760
the frenzy of foresight.

ANTISTROPHE

Upon the battle towers of Troy,
around her walls, Trojans will stand
when Ares in harness of bronze
on these stately ships over the sea   765
approaches the runnels of Simois.
Yes, he'll come desiring to seize Helen
to hale her from Priam's palace—   770
she whose brothers are the Dioscuri in heaven—
back to the land of Greece
by toil of battle
and the shields and spears of Achaeans.

EPODE

Pergamum with walls of stone, Phrygia's town,
he will encircle in bloody battle,   775
to drag their bodies headless away;°
then from the citadel's top peak to earth
he will sack all the dwellings in Troy city.
So every maiden will wail loudly,
and with them Priam's queen.   780

And Helen too, who is daughter of Zeus,
she will cry aloud
for having forsaken her husband.
May this worry never be ours   785
or that of our children's children!
To be as the golden Lydian ladies,
or the Phrygian wives—
to stand before their looms
and wail to one another:
"Who will lay hands on my shining hair,   790
when tears flood my eyes,
and who will pluck me like a flower°
out of my country's ruin?"
Oh, it is on account of you,
child of the arch-necked swan,
if the story is to be believed,
the story that Leda bore you to a winged bird,   795
to Zeus himself transformed!
But perhaps this is a fable
from the book of the Muses
borne to me out of season,   800
a senseless tale.

(Enter Achilles from the side.)

ACHILLES

Where is the commander-in-chief?
Will one of his aides give him this message—
that Achilles, the son of Peleus, is here
at the door of his pavilion.

    This delay by the river Euripus
is not alike for all, let me tell you.
Some of us are unmarried. We've simply   805
abandoned our halls and sit here idly
on the beaches. Others have left at home
their wives and children, all because
a terrible passion has seized all Greece

to make this expedition—not without
heaven's contrivance.

                    Whatever others
may argue, I'll tell my righteous grievance!   810
I left Pharsalia and my father Peleus,
and here by the gentle Euripus I must wait
and curb my own troops, my Myrmidons.
They are forever urging me and saying:
"Why do we wait? How many weeks must we   815
drag out before we head for Troy? Act, if
you're going to act! If not, then wait no longer
on Atreus' sons and on their dallyings,
but lead the army home."

                    (Enter Clytemnestra from the tent.)

CLYTEMNESTRA
Son of the Nereid, I come to greet you—
I heard your voice inside the tent.   820

ACHILLES
O queenly modesty—whom do I see,
a woman peerless in her loveliness?

CLYTEMNESTRA
It is not surprising that you do not know me
since into my presence you never came before.
But I praise your respect for modesty.

ACHILLES
Who are you? And why, lady, have you come   825
to the mustering-in of the Greek army—
you, a woman, into a camp of armed men?

CLYTEMNESTRA
I am the daughter of Leda, Clytemnestra.
Agamemnon is my husband.

ACHILLES
                    My lady,

you have said well and briefly what was fitting.
But I may not rightly hold converse here   830
with you or any woman.

(He starts to exit to the side.)

CLYTEMNESTRA

Oh wait! Why rush away? With your
right hand clasp mine and let this be
the beginning of a blest betrothal.

ACHILLES

What are you saying? I take your hand in mine?
That's wrong—I'd be ashamed before the king.

CLYTEMNESTRA

It is wholly right, child of the Nereid,   835
since soon you will marry my daughter.

ACHILLES

                    What!
What marriage do you speak of, my lady?
I have no word to put into my answer,
unless this I say—from some strange frenzy
of your mind you have conceived this story.

CLYTEMNESTRA

By nature all men are shy, seeing new
kinsmen, or hearing talk of marriage.   840

ACHILLES

My lady, never have I courted your daughter,
or from the sons of Atreus either
has ever word of this marriage come to me.

CLYTEMNESTRA

I do not understand—I am amazed at your words.

ACHILLES

Let's search this out together, for there may   845
be error in what we both have said.

CLYTEMNESTRA

Have I been horribly abused?
The betrothal which I came here to find,
at Aulis, never existed here or anywhere
but is a lie—oh, I am crushed with shame!

ACHILLES

My lady, perhaps it is only this:
someone is laughing at us both.
But I beg of you: take any mockery
without concern, and bear it lightly.   850

CLYTEMNESTRA

Farewell! Deceived as I am, humiliated,
I can no longer lift my eyes to yours.

ACHILLES

I too bid you farewell, my lady,
and go now into the tent to seek your husband.

(The Old Man appears at the door of the tent.)

OLD MAN

Sir, wait! I'm calling to you there—O   855
grandson of Aeacus, child of the goddess,
and you, my lady, daughter of Leda!

ACHILLES

Who shouts through the open door—and in terror?

OLD MAN

I am a slave. I cannot boast to you
of my position—that is my fate.

ACHILLES

Whose slave? Not mine; he would not be here
in Agamemnon's retinue.

OLD MAN
                    I belong

to the lady who stands before this tent—   860
a gift to her from her father, Tyndareus.

ACHILLES

I wait. Now say why you stop me here.

OLD MAN

Are both of you alone before the doors?

ACHILLES

We are. Speak and come out from the royal tent.

(The Old Man now completes his entrance from the door of the tent.)

OLD MAN

May Fate and my good foresight rescue you!

ACHILLES

Your story's for the future.° But you're so slow!   865

CLYTEMNESTRA

Speak, old man, don't wait to kiss my hand.

OLD MAN

You know who I am, my lady, loyal
to you and to your children?

CLYTEMNESTRA

                              Yes, I know,
you are an old house servant in the palace.

OLD MAN

King Agamemnon took me as a portion
in your dowry.

CLYTEMNESTRA

                    Yes, yes, and coming to Argos   870
with us, you have been mine ever since.

OLD MAN

That is the truth, and I am more loyal
to you than to your husband.

CLYTEMNESTRA

　　　　　　Now the mystery
you have been guarding, out with it!

OLD MAN

I'll tell you quickly. Her father plans
with his own hand to kill your child . . .

CLYTEMNESTRA

What words of a crazed mind
have come out of your mouth, old man!

OLD MAN

. . . with a bloody knife at her white throat.   875
He will kill her.

CLYTEMNESTRA

　　　　　　Oh, how miserable am I!
He has been stricken, then, with madness?

OLD MAN

No. In all other things, my queen,
your lord is sane except in this regard,
toward you and toward the child.

CLYTEMNESTRA

Why? Why? What is the demon of vengeance
which drives him to this horror?

OLD MAN

The oracle of Calchas: that the fleet may sail . . .

CLYTEMNESTRA

Her father will kill her! O poor me, poor child!   880
You say the fleet? Where will it sail?

OLD MAN

. . . to the lords of Troy and to their halls,
so that Menelaus may bring Helen back.

CLYTEMNESTRA

Oh, fate then has bound Helen's homecoming
to my daughter and to her death.

OLD MAN

You know all of the mystery now, and that
it is to Artemis that her father
will sacrifice the child.

CLYTEMNESTRA

And the marriage,
was that a pretext which he invented
to bring me from Argos?

OLD MAN

Yes, for the king
calculated that you would bring her gladly   885
to be the bride of Achilles.

CLYTEMNESTRA

O daughter,
we have been brought here, you and with you
your mother, to death and to destruction.

OLD MAN

The fate of the child is pitiable
and yours too, my queen. The king
has dared a deed of horror.

CLYTEMNESTRA

Now, I cannot
hold them back, these streams of tears. I am lost,
utterly.

OLD MAN

What greater cause, my lady,
for grieving than a child taken away?
Weep, weep.

CLYTEMNESTRA

These plans—how do you know them   890

for the truth? Where did you find out these things,
old man?

OLD MAN

I'll tell you. I was on my way, running
to bring you a letter, a second to
follow the first from my lord Agamemnon.

CLYTEMNESTRA

Forbidding me to bring the girl to death—
or confirming?

OLD MAN

No. He said not to bring her,
for this second time he wrote sanely and
in his right mind.

CLYTEMNESTRA

Then why didn't you deliver that letter?

OLD MAN

Because Menelaus tore it out of my hand,   895
and he is the cause of all our ruin.

CLYTEMNESTRA

Child of the Nereid, Peleus' son, do you hear?

ACHILLES

I hear the story of your fate and misery
and I cannot bear my part in it.

CLYTEMNESTRA

They use this trick of your marriage
to slaughter my child!

ACHILLES

Now lady, let me
add my own reproach upon your husband.

CLYTEMNESTRA

Oh, you were born of a goddess, I—
I am mortal so I am not ashamed   900

to clasp your knees. Why should I put on airs?
Or what should matter more to me
than my own daughter? Please, oh goddess-born,
protect us both—me from my evil fate,
and her who is called your wife, even if she's not.
It was for your sake that I led her here,
to be your wife, and crowned her head   905
with a bride's wreath.

               Oh, I have brought her here,
I now discover, not for marrying,
but to be killed! A shameful reproach
will be yours if you do not shield her!
Although no marriage yokes you
to the unhappy girl, yet in name at least
you were called her lord and her dear husband.
Listen to me—since through your name   910
you have brought my undoing and my end,
I beg you, by your chin, your right hand, and
by your mother—O cleanse your name of this reproach!

     Child of the goddess, I have no altar
to which I can flee for safety except
to your knees, and I have no friend near by.
You've heard the savage and shameless plans
of Agamemnon the king, and you see
how I have come, a woman and helpless,
into a camp of men, sailors of the fleet,
eager for any violence and yet
strong to save and help if it come
into their hearts. Oh—if you have the courage,   915
now stretch out your hand and surely I am
saved, but if you do not dare it—I am lost!

CHORUS LEADER
   Oh, what a power is motherhood, possessing
   a potent spell. All people alike
   fight fiercely for their children.

ACHILLES

At your words in pride and in anger
my soul is aroused. And yet I've learned to curb   920
my vaunting spirit, when I face disaster,
just as I don't immoderately rejoice
when triumphs come. Certainly a man schooled
well in reason may have hope to live
his life successfully. At times, of course,
it's pleasant not to be overwise; but too,
other times there are when intelligence is useful.   925
I was educated by the most god-fearing
of all, by Chiron, and it was from him
I've learned to act in singleness of heart.
Our generals, the Atreidae, I obey
when their command is righteous, but
when evil, I shall not obey, and here
as in Troy I shall show my nature free   930
to fight my enemy with honor.

   But you, lady, suffer things savage and cruel
from those you love, and so with my compassion
I shall protect you all around like a shield
as far as a young man may.
I tell you—never will your daughter   935
who is my betrothed die murdered by
her father's hand. Nor to this conspiracy
of your husband will I offer myself.
For though my sword remains undrawn, my name
will kill your child—and all your husband's fault.
Then I would be defiled if through me   940
and through my marriage the maiden dies!
Then in dishonor, undeserved, incredible,
she'd suffer intolerable wrongs.

   It will seem I've been the basest of all Greeks,
no more a man than Menelaus,   945
no son of Peleus but a fiend's child,
if for your husband's sake my name does murder.

No! By Nereus, fostered by ocean's
waves, by the father of Thetis who bore me,
by him I swear, never will King Agamemnon
lay hands upon your daughter—no, nor even   950
touch with his fingertips her robe. For otherwise
Mount Sipylus, that bastion of barbarians,
from which our generals' lineage derives,
will be famed, while my Phthia is unknown.
When Calchas next makes sacrifice he'll find   955
bitter the barley and the holy water.
What sort of man is a prophet? Let me tell you.
When lucky, he guesses a few things right;
but mostly he utters lies, and then like smoke
he disappears.
Now must I tell you, it is not on account
of this marriage I have said these things—
no, there are many girls who'd marry me,   960
but I cannot endure the insult and injury
which the lord Agamemnon has heaped upon me!
What would have been fitting, if he had wanted
to snare his daughter, then he should
have asked of me if he could use my name.
For what convinced Clytemnestra to give
her daughter was that I would be the husband.
I would have granted this to him, the use   965
of my name for the sake of Greece
if it were the only way that we could sail.
I wouldn't have denied my help to the common cause
of those with whom I march.
                              But now
I am nothing and nobody in the eyes
of the army chiefs! At their convenience
they do me honor or injury. I tell you:
if anyone tries to rob me of your daughter
then before I go to Troy I'll stain this sword
with his barbarian blood.   970

But you, lady,
be calm now and comforted. I show myself
to you now as though I were a mighty god;
and though I am no god, someday I'll be one.

CHORUS LEADER

You have spoken, Peleus' son, words worthy   975
of yourself and of the dread sea goddess.

CLYTEMNESTRA

How can I praise and yet not overpraise,
or stint my words and lose your graciousness?
The noble, when they're praised, to some extent
hate those who laud them—if they laud too much.   980
    I am ashamed to tell my piteous story;
the affliction is mine, not yours—
and yet, a good man, though he be far
from the unfortunate, will succor them.
Have pity—my sorrow is worthy of it.   985
For first I thought that you would be my son,
and cherished in my heart an empty dream!
But now death threatens my child, an ill omen
for your own future marriage! So
you must protect yourself as well as me!
Your opening words were fine, the last ones too.   990
My daughter will be rescued if you will.
    Do you desire that she come to clasp your knees?
It would transgress a maiden's character,
but if you wish it she will put aside
her modesty and come out from this tent.
But if I can win you without her coming,   995
she shall remain indoors. We always should
reverence modesty, if circumstance permits.

ACHILLES

Oh, do not bring her here for me to see!
Let us avoid foolish scandal, for the troops

being crowded, idle, and away from home, 1000
love filthy gossip and foul talk.
If your daughter comes a suppliant, or never,
it is the same. This enterprise is mine—
believe my words—to rid you of these evils. 1005
Oh, may I die if I speak false in this
and only live if I shall save the girl!

CLYTEMNESTRA
Heaven bless you for helping the unfortunate.

ACHILLES
Listen to me and we'll succeed in this.

CLYTEMNESTRA
What do you mean? I must listen to you. 1010

ACHILLES
Then once more let us persuade her father
to a saner mood.

CLYTEMNESTRA
                    He is a coward,
and in terror of the army.

ACHILLES
                    Reason can wrestle
and overthrow terror.

CLYTEMNESTRA
                    My hopes are cold on that.
What must I do?

ACHILLES
First this, beseech him like a suppliant 1015
not to kill his daughter. If he resists
then come to me you must. But if he yields
to your appeal—why then
I need not be a party to this affair.
His very yielding will mean her salvation.
So, if I act by reason and not violence,

I'll be a better friend and, too, escape   1020
the troops' reproach. So without me you and°
those dear to you may succeed in all.

CLYTEMNESTRA

You've spoken wisely. What seems good to you
I'll do. But if we fail in what I want,   1025
where can I find and see you once again,
in desperation seeking your hand and help?

ACHILLES

I'll be on watch just like a sentinel.
But we'll appoint a place—and so avoid
your frantic search among the troops for me.   1030
Do nothing to demean your heritage;
Tyndareus' house deserves a fair report;
his is a high name among all Greeks.

CLYTEMNESTRA

These things shall be as you have spoken them.
Rule me—it is my obligation to obey.
If there are gods,° you, being righteous,
will win reward; if not, why toil in vain?   1035

(Exit Clytemnestra into the tent and Achilles to the side.)

CHORUS [*singing*]

STROPHE

Oh what bridal song with Libyan pipe,
with lyre dance-loving,
with reeds pipe-pealing,
rang forth on the air,
when to Pelion came lovely-haired   1040
the Muses to the feast of the gods—
gold-sandaled their feet
stamping the ground
to the marriage of Peleus,
over the hills of the Centaurs,
down through Pelion's woodlands,

to magnify with music's praise   1045
Thetis and the son of Aeacus.
And Phrygian Ganymede, Dardanus' child,   1050
of Zeus favored and loved,
from mixing bowls into golden cups
poured the libation, while
on the glistening sea sands, circling,   1055
the fifty daughters of Nereus
wove the marriage dance.

ANTISTROPHE

With lances of pine and leafy crowns
the reveling band of horse-riding Centaurs came   1060
to the gods' feast and the bowls brimming
with Bacchus' gift.
Wildly they cried, "Hail, Nereus' daughter,
hail to the son you will bear! He will be a bright light blazing
for Thessaly—so says the prophet
of Phoebus' songs, foreknowing,   1065
Chiron. He will come with an army
of Myrmidons, spear throwers,
into famous Troyland to sack   1070
Priam's glorious city.
And he will put upon his body
the golden armor wrought by Hephaestus,
gift of his goddess mother,
Thetis who bore him."   1075
So the gods blessed the marriage
then of Peleus, noble in birth,
and of the first
of Nereus' daughters.

EPODE

But you, Iphigenia, upon your head   1080
and on your lovely hair
will the Argives wreathe a crown
for sacrifice,

as on a heifer, dappled, unblemished,°
that has come down from the hill caves—
they will drench your mortal throat with blood.
You were not reared   1085
by the music
of a herdsman's pipe
but by your mother's side,
fostered to marry a son of Inachus.
Oh, where now has the countenance
of Modesty or Virtue   1090
any strength,
when the blasphemer rules,
and heedless men
thrust Virtue behind them,
when Lawlessness rules law,   1095
and no man competes with his neighbor
to avoid the ill-will of the gods?

                    (Enter Clytemnestra from the tent.)

CLYTEMNESTRA

I have come from the pavilion seeking
my husband. For he left our tent
and has been absent long. My unhappy
child now weeps her heart out, first moaning   1100
soft, then crying aloud, for she has heard
of the death her father plots against her—
I speak of Agamemnon, and he comes. Now
in an instant he will be found guilty
of this unholy crime against his child!   1105

                    (Enter Agamemnon from the side.)

AGAMEMNON

O daughter of Leda, I am glad
to find you now outside our tent,
for at this moment I must speak to you
of several things not proper for a bride to hear.

CLYTEMNESTRA

What things fit so perfectly for you
this moment?

AGAMEMNON

Send for the child from the pavilion   1110
to join her father. But first listen to me:
the lustral waters have now been prepared
and the barley to throw on cleansing fire;
victims—heifers—are ready, their black blood
soon to flow in honor of Artemis.

CLYTEMNESTRA

As you speak, you give these things fair names.   1115
But for the deed of your intention—
I can find no good name for that.

(Calling into the tent.)

Come outside, my daughter; the intentions
of your father you now know fully and well.
Come and bring your brother Orestes,
child, and cover him with your robe.

(Enter Iphigenia from the tent, carrying Orestes.)

Behold she is here, and in her coming   1120
to you now she is obedient. But as to the rest
of this business, on her behalf and mine
I shall now speak.

AGAMEMNON

Child, why do you cry
and look at me no longer with delight?
Why do you look upon the ground and hood
your eyes from me with your robe?

CLYTEMNESTRA

I do not know
how I can make a beginning of my story

to you, since everything can serve me as

beginning or as middle or as end.

AGAMEMNON

What has happened?

Why do you both look at me with trouble

and with terror in your eyes?

CLYTEMNESTRA

My husband,

answer my question with the courage of a man.

AGAMEMNON

Go on—I am willing. There is no need

to command an answer from me.

CLYTEMNESTRA

Your child and mine—do you intend to kill her?

AGAMEMNON

What?

What a horrible thing to say! Such suspicions

are utterly inappropriate!

CLYTEMNESTRA

Calm down! Just give me an answer to that question.

AGAMEMNON

A reasonable question I will answer reasonably.

CLYTEMNESTRA

I ask no other question. Answer this one.

AGAMEMNON

Oh fate! Misfortune! Oh the god that rules me!

CLYTEMNESTRA

You? Me and her! One evil fate

rules three and brings great misery for us all.

AGAMEMNON

What wrong has been done to you?

CLYTEMNESTRA

             You can ask me this?
That mind of yours seems pretty mindless!

AGAMEMNON

  I am destroyed—my secret is betrayed. 1140

CLYTEMNESTRA

  Listen, I know exactly what it is
  you mean to do to me. And now your silence
  and these groans of yours show that you admit it.
  So do not labor to speak at length.

AGAMEMNON

                 Then see,
  I'm silent. For me to lie would only add 1145
  shamelessness to all of my misfortune.

CLYTEMNESTRA

  Hear me now—
  for I shall give you open speech and no
  dark sayings or enigmas any more.
      And this reproach I first hurl in your teeth,
  that I married you against my will, after
  you murdered Tantalus, my first husband, 1150
  and dashed my living babe upon the earth,°
  brutally tearing him from my breasts.
  And then, the two sons of Zeus, my brothers,
  on horseback came and in bright armor made
  war upon you. Till you got upon your knees
  to my old father, Tyndareus, and he 1155
  rescued you. So you kept me for your bed.
      But after that I became reconciled
  to you and to your house, and you will bear
  witness that I, as your wife, have been
  blameless, modest in passion, and in honor
  seeking to increase your house so that 1160

your coming-in had gladness and
your going-out joy. A rare spoil for a man
is the winning of a good wife; very
plentiful are the worthless women.
And so I bore you this son and three daughters.
Now one of these you tear away from me.   1165
If any man should ask you why, why
do you kill your daughter? What answer will
you make? Or must your words come from my mouth?
"So Menelaus can get his Helen back."
And so you pay our child as the price
for an evil woman, buying with what you love
the most a creature loathed above all others.   1170

But think now. If you leave me and go
to this war, and if your absence there
from me is stretched over the years,
with what heart shall I keep your halls in Argos?
With what heart look at her chair and find it
empty of her; at her maiden chamber   1175
and it empty always; and when I sit
alone with tears of loneliness and for
a mourning that will have no end?
                              "O child!"
I shall then cry out. "Who brought you to this death?
It was your father—he and no other,
and by no other's hand!"
                         This is the hatred,
Agamemnon, and the retribution
you leave in your house.° Here am I
and the children you have left to me.
But little more do we need of pretext   1180
and provocation so that upon your
homecoming we give you the welcome that
is wholly due. No! by the gods, do not
force me to become a woman of evil!

And you, do not become evil yourself!

Well: after the sacrifice of your child, what prayer   1185
can your mouth utter? What things of good for you
will you be praying for while you cut her throat?
Perhaps an evil coming home, to match
this vile departure? Tell me, in all
conscience, how can I ask the gods to give
you any blessing? We must think the gods
fools, if we ask blessing for the killers   1190
of our children!

When you return at last
to Argos, after the war, will you embrace
your children? That would be a sacrilege!
What child of yours will look you in the face,
so you can drag one off for sacrifice?

Speak to me—have you ever taken account
of such things in any way? Or is your thought,
your need, only to brandish scepters and   1195
lead armies? Well then, here is a righteous
offer you should make to the Greek army:
"Achaeans, you are eager to sail for Troy—
then cast lots to find whose daughter must die!"
This would be justice—rather than offer
your own child, as victim to the army.   1200
Or let Menelaus—for this is his affair—
kill his own daughter for her mother's sake.
For look, my girl is torn from me, from me
who have been faithful to my marriage,
but she who has sinned against her husband's bed—
she will return to prosper, and keep her daughter   1205
safe at home.

And now at last you tell me
if in anything I have failed to speak
justly. But if my words are fair and right,
then do not kill our girl but act with sense.

Agamemnon, yield to her! It is good to save
a child's life. No one will contradict that.   1210

IPHIGENIA

O my father—if I had the tongue of Orpheus
so that I could charm with song the stones to
leap and follow me, or if my words could
quite beguile anyone I wished—I'd use
my magic now. But only with tears can I   1215
make arguments and here I offer them.
O Father, my dear mother bore my body,
and now it is a suppliant's, tight clinging
to your knees. Do not take away this life
of mine before its dying time. Nor make me
go down under the earth to see the world
of darkness, for it is sweet to look on
the day's light.

     I was first to call you father,   1220
you to call me child. And of your children
first to sit upon your knees. How happy
we both were in our love! "O child,"
you said, "surely one day I shall see you
happy in your husband's home, and like
a flower blooming for me and in my honor."   1225
Then as I clung to you and wove my fingers
in your beard, I answered, "Father, you,
old and reverend then, with love shall I
receive you into my home, and so repay you
for the years of trouble and your fostering   1230
care of me." I have in memory all these words
of yours and mine. But you, forgetting,
have willed it in your heart to kill me.

     Oh no—by Pelops
and by Atreus, your father, and

by my mother who suffered travail
at my birth and now must suffer a second   1235
time for me! Oh, oh—the marriage
of Paris and Helen—why must it touch
my life? Why must Paris be my ruin?
Father, look at me, and into my eyes;
kiss me, so that if my words fail,   1240
and if I die, this thing of love I may
hold in my heart and remember.

                                            (To Orestes.)

    My brother, so little can you help us
who love you, but weep with me and
beg our father not to kill your sister.
Oh, the threat of evil is instinct,
even in an infant's heart. See, even
without speech, he begs you, Father,   1245
so pity and have mercy on my life.
Yes, both of us beseech you, this little child
and I, your daughter grown. Now these words
will conquer any argument: to see
the light of day is sweet for everyone;   1250
the shadow world below is nothing.
People are mad, I say, who pray for death;
it is better that we live ever so
miserably than die in glory.

CHORUS LEADER
    O wicked Helen, through you, and through your
    marriages, this terrible ordeal has come
    to the sons of Atreus and to their children.

AGAMEMNON
    I know what calls for pity and I know   1255
    what does not. And I love my children!
    Did I not I would be mad indeed.
    Terrible it is to me, my girl, to dare

this thing. But terrible also not to dare it.

      For in either case my fate will be the same.
Behold the armies, girt about by the fleet,
with all their bronzen armor at their feet—   1260
none of them can sail to Ilium's towers
nor sack the famous bastion of Troy°   1263
until, as the prophet Calchas has decreed,   1262
I make you the victim of this sacrifice.
O child, a mighty passion seizes
the Greek soldiers and maddens them to sail
with utmost speed to that barbarian place   1265
that they may halt the rape of our Greek women.
The army, angered, will come to Argos,
slaughter my daughters, murder you all and me
if I annul the divine oracle
of the goddess. It is not Menelaus
making a slave of me—nor am I here
at Menelaus' will, but Greece lays upon me   1270
this sacrifice of you beyond all will
of mine. It's Greece that rules me.
           O my child,
Greece turns to you, to me, and now,
as much as in us lies she must be free;
and never by the barbarians in their violence
must Greeks be robbed of their wives.   1275

(Exit Agamemnon to the side.)

CLYTEMNESTRA [*chanting*]
   O maidens who are friendly to us—O my child,
   what a terrible dying is yours.
   Your father, betraying you to death,
   has fled away.

IPHIGENIA [*chanting*]
   Oh, pitiable am I, Mother!
   The selfsame grieving song

is ours, fallen from fate's hands.   1280
Life is no longer mine,
nor the dayspring's splendor.

[now singing]
O snow-beaten Phrygian glen and Ida's
hill: there on a day was the tender suckling thrown,   1285
Priam's child, from his mother torn,
for the doom of death; it was the herdsman
of Ida, Paris of Ida,
so named, so named in his Trojan city.   1290
Would they had never reared him,
reared Alexander, herdsman of cattle,
to dwell by the silvery waters,
by the nymphs and their fountains,   1295
by that meadow green and abundant
with roses and hyacinths
gathered for goddesses!
There on that day came Pallas   1300
and Cypris the beguiling,
Hera, and Hermes, Zeus' messenger°—
Cypris, who dominates with desire,
Pallas with her spear,   1305
and Hera, Zeus' royal wife and queen—
they came for the judging,
for the hateful battle of beauty
which to me brings death, O maidens,
but to the Danaan girls glory.   1310
O my mother, my mother,
Artemis has seized me, for Ilium
a first sacrifice!
He who began my life
has betrayed me in misery
to a lonely dying.
Oh, my wretchedness,   1315
I saw her,

Helen, doom-starred and evil;
bitter, bitter
is the death you bring me!
Murdered by my father—
accursed butchery,
for I shall be slain
by his unholy hands.
Oh, if only Aulis had not taken   1320
to the bosom of her harborage
these, our ships,
with their beaks of bronze!
Oh, if only
the breath of Zeus had not swept them
to the roadstead that faces the narrows.
Zeus' breath—it brings delight
and doom to mortals;   1325
at one time the sails laugh
in a favoring breeze,
at another, Zeus the Almighty
blows down upon mortals
delay and doom.
O toil-bearing race, O toil-bearing   1330
creatures living for a day—
fate finds for every man
his share of misery.
O Tyndareus' daughter,
what burden you have laid
upon the Danaans   1335
of anguish and disaster!

CHORUS LEADER [*now speaking*]
  I pity you for your evil fate. Oh—
  that it had never found you out!

IPHIGENIA
  O Mother, there are men—I see them coming here.

CLYTEMNESTRA
　　It is Achilles, son of the goddess
　　for whom your father brought you here.

IPHIGENIA
　　Servants, open the doors, so that I may　　　　　　　1340
　　hide myself.

CLYTEMNESTRA
　　　　　　Why do you run away, child?

IPHIGENIA
　　I am ashamed to see him—to look
　　On the face of Achilles.

CLYTEMNESTRA
　　　　　　But why?

IPHIGENIA
　　Oh, my unlucky marriage—I am ashamed!

CLYTEMNESTRA
　　In this crisis, daughter, you can't afford
　　these delicate feelings. Stay—this is no time
　　for modesty if we can hope for help.

(Enter Achilles from the side, with armor-bearers.)

ACHILLES
　　Woman of misery and misfortune,　　　　　　　　　　1345
　　Leda's daughter . . .

CLYTEMNESTRA
　　　　　　Yes, you have said what is true.
　　I am she.

ACHILLES
　　　　　　. . . the Argives are shouting
　　a thing of terror . . .

CLYTEMNESTRA

What are they shouting?
Tell me!

ACHILLES

... about your daughter ...

CLYTEMNESTRA

Oh, these words
Of ill omen!

ACHILLES

... that she must be slaughtered
in sacrifice.

CLYTEMNESTRA

And was there no one
on the other side to argue against them?°

ACHILLES

Yes, I spoke to the yelling crowd and so
was in danger ...

CLYTEMNESTRA

In danger of what?

ACHILLES

... of death by stoning.

CLYTEMNESTRA

Oh—because you
tried to save my child?   1350

ACHILLES

Yes, for that.

CLYTEMNESTRA

But who would have dared to lay a hand on you?

ACHILLES

Every Greek soldier.

CLYTEMNESTRA
                    But your own legion
of Myrmidons, they were there at your side?

ACHILLES
And the first to threaten my death.

CLYTEMNESTRA
                    O my child—
now we are lost.

ACHILLES
                    They mocked me, they shouted
that I had become a slave of this marriage.

CLYTEMNESTRA
    What did you say?

ACHILLES
                    I answered that they
must never slaughter my bride . . .   1355

CLYTEMNESTRA
                    Oh, a right answer!

ACHILLES
    . . . whom her father had pledged to me for marriage.

CLYTEMNESTRA
    Yes, and brought to you from Argos.

ACHILLES
    They drowned my voice by their yelling
and cried me down.

CLYTEMNESTRA
                    Oh, the mob—what a terror
and an evil!

ACHILLES
                    Nonetheless I will defend you!

CLYTEMNESTRA

You—one man fighting a thousand!

ACHILLES

Look!
These men are bringing me armor for that battle.

CLYTEMNESTRA

May the gods bless your courage!

ACHILLES

I shall be blest!

CLYTEMNESTRA

The child then shall not be killed?   1360

ACHILLES

Not if I live!

CLYTEMNESTRA

But tell me now, who will come here and try
to seize the girl?

ACHILLES

Men by thousands will come—
Odysseus will lead them.

CLYTEMNESTRA

Sisyphus' son?

ACHILLES

Yes!

CLYTEMNESTRA

Of his own will, or chosen by the army?

ACHILLES

He will be chosen, but glad of his appointment.

CLYTEMNESTRA

Chosen for evil, for bloodshed and murder!

ACHILLES

But I will keep him from the girl!   1365

CLYTEMNESTRA

Will he, if she resists, drag her away?

ACHILLES

There is no doubt—and by her golden hair!

CLYTEMNESTRA

What must I do then?

ACHILLES

Hold fast to the child!

CLYTEMNESTRA

And so save her from murder!

ACHILLES

It comes to this.

IPHIGENIA

Mother, now listen to my words. I see   *Sudden*
your soul in anger against your husband.   *Change*
This is a foolish and an evil rage.
Oh, I know when we stand before a helpless
doom how hard it is to bear.   1370
                    But hear me now.
It is rightful and good that we thank and
praise our friend for his eager kindness.
But you must be careful and see that he
is not blamed by the army. Such a thing
would win us nothing but would bring him
utter ruin.
                    And now hear me, Mother,
what thought has seized me and I have conceived
in my heart. I shall die—I am resolved—   1375
and having fixed my mind I want to die
well and gloriously, putting away

from me whatever is weak and ignoble.
Listen to me, Mother, follow my words
and tell me if I speak well. All Greece turns
her eyes to me, to me only, great Greece
in her might. Through me alone is sailing
for the fleet, through me the sack and overthrow
of Troy. Because of me, never more will
barbarians wrong and ravish Greek women,   1380
drag them from happiness and their homes
in Hellas. The penalty will be paid
fully for Paris' rape of Helen.

           And all
these things, all of them, my death will achieve
and accomplish. I, savior of Greece,
will win honor and my name shall be blessed.

    It is wrong for me to love life too deeply.   1385
You bore me, Mother, for all of Greece,
not for yourself alone. Wrong and injury
our country suffers, and so thousands
of men arm themselves, thousands more in these ships
pick up their oars. They will dare very greatly
against the enemy and die for Greece.
Shall my one life prevent all this? Where is   1390
the judgment of justice here? To the soldiers
who die is there a word we can answer?

    But now consider further. Is it right
for this man to make war upon all the Greeks
for one woman's sake and surely die?
Far better that ten thousand women die
if this keep one man only facing the light
and alive.

        O Mother, if Artemis
wishes to take the life of my body,   1395
shall I, who am mortal, oppose
the divine will? No—that is unthinkable!
To Greece I give this body of mine.

[161] IPHIGENIA IN AULIS

Slay it in sacrifice and conquer Troy.
These things coming to pass, Mother, will be
a remembrance for you. They will be
my children, my marriage—through the years
my good name and my glory. It is right
that Greeks rule the barbarians, not barbarians   1400
the Greeks. For they are slaves, and we are free.

Greece vs. barbarians

CHORUS LEADER
  Child, you play your part with nobleness.
  The fault is with the goddess and with fate.

ACHILLES
              O child of Agamemnon—
  if I had won you as my bride, if only—   1405
  I would have sworn a god had given me
  happiness. I envy Greece because you
  are hers, not mine. And you too I envy
  for Greece's sake. You've spoken beautifully,
  and worthily of our country. You won't fight
  against god's will. You chose the thing that was
  good and was fated. And all the more I
  see of your nature—for it is noble—
  desire for our marriage overcomes   1410
  my spirit.
              Listen to me, listen.
  For I want to serve you and help you. Yes,
  and to carry you home as my bride.
  O Thetis, goddess mother, witness this
  is the truth. I am in agony to throw
  myself into battle with all the Greeks
  to save you. Consider again how
  terrible a thing and how evil is death!   1415

IPHIGENIA
  I speak this as one past hope and fear,°
  so listen to me. It is enough that
  Helen, daughter of Tyndareus, because

of her body hurls men into war
and to slaughter. But you, stranger and my friend,
you must not die for me or kill any man;
only let me, if I have the strength, save Greece.   1420

ACHILLES

O noble heart! How can I ever add
words of mine to these of yours, since you
have fixed your will to die. Your soul is noble—
who would not speak this truth? But yet—it is
possible you will repent and alter
your fixed mind. Then know my proposal   1425
and offer—I shall go with these arms and
shall place them by the altar directly
in order that I can prevent your death.
Perhaps you'll want to follow my advice
even at the final second when you
see the sword thrust at your throat. For this is
a rash and hasty impulse; I will not   1430
let you die for it. So, I shall arrive
with these arms at the goddess' altar,
and there wait and watch till you come.

                              (*Exit Achilles to the side.*)

IPHIGENIA

You make no sound, but you are weeping, Mother.
Why do you weep for me?

CLYTEMNESTRA

                    Is not this sorrow
terrible enough to break my heart?

IPHIGENIA

Stop! And trust me in all of this, Mother.   1435
Do not make a coward of me.

CLYTEMNESTRA

                    Daughter,

I do not want to wrong or hurt you.
Tell me what I must do.

IPHIGENIA

Here is one thing I ask:
don't shear from your head the lock of hair
or dress yourself in mourning for my sake.

CLYTEMNESTRA

What are you saying, child? When I have lost
you forever!

IPHIGENIA

No! I am not lost
but saved! And you too, through me, will be   1440
remembered gloriously.

CLYTEMNESTRA

Oh, what do you mean?
Is it not right that I mourn your death?

IPHIGENIA

No! For I say no funeral mound is
to be heaped up for me.

CLYTEMNESTRA

What? Isn't it
ordained and rightful that there be a burying
for the dead?

IPHIGENIA

The altar of the goddess
who is Zeus' daughter—that will be
my grave and my monument.

CLYTEMNESTRA

O my child,
yours are the good words and the right ones.   1445
I will obey you.

IPHIGENIA

That will be my memorial
as one favored by fate because I brought
help to Greece.

CLYTEMNESTRA

Your sisters—what message
shall I take them?

IPHIGENIA

O Mother, do not dress
them in mourning.

CLYTEMNESTRA

But have you some last word
of love that I may speak to them?

IPHIGENIA

Only this—
I say good-bye to them now. That is all.
Orestes—do this, nurture him and see   1450
that he comes to strength and manhood for my sake.

CLYTEMNESTRA

Embrace and look at him for the last time.

IPHIGENIA   *(To Orestes.)*

Dearest—you tried to help me as best you could!

CLYTEMNESTRA

O my child, when I go home to Argos
is there something I can do to bring you joy?

IPHIGENIA

Yes. Do not hate him. Do not hate my father
who is your husband.

CLYTEMNESTRA

Oh! Oh! Your father

must run a course of agony and terror
for your sake.

IPHIGENIA

Acting against his will,
for the sake of Greece, he has committed me
to death.

CLYTEMNESTRA

By a treacherous plot! Unkingly
and unworthy of Atreus!

IPHIGENIA

Who will lead me
to the altar, before they seize me
and drag me by my hair?

CLYTEMNESTRA

I—I will come with you . . .

IPHIGENIA

No, no, that is wrong!

CLYTEMNESTRA

. . . holding with my hand
to your robe.

IPHIGENIA

Mother, trust me,
here you must stay, which will be better
for you and for me also. Let it be
one of my father's attendants who brings me
to the meadow of Artemis and to the place
where I shall be killed.

CLYTEMNESTRA

Oh, child,
are you going now?

IPHIGENIA

        Yes.
And not to come back again.

CLYTEMNESTRA

        Leaving your mother?   1465

IPHIGENIA

You see how undeserved.

CLYTEMNESTRA

        Oh, stay.
Don't leave me, child!

IPHIGENIA

Stop! I forbid your crying out or any tears!
O women, lift your voices up to Artemis,
in honor of my fate and of my dying
shout a loud paean of glory to Zeus' daughter.
And let the host of Danaans be silent,
let the ritual basket be prepared,   1470
let the fire blaze with holy barley.
And let my father circle to the right
around the altar. For it is to bring the Greeks
salvation and triumph that I now depart.

[*singing*]
Lead me on
for the sack and overthrowing   1475
of Troy city
and the Phrygian land.
Put on my hair a wreath
of garlands,
O drench me with the waters
of purification.
About the altar of Artemis,
about her temple,
dance!

Let us dance in honor of Artemis, 1480
goddess, queen and blest.
With my own blood
in sacrifice
I will wash out
the fated curse of the gods.
O Mother, my lady mother, 1485
I shall give you no tears
for when I come to the holy place
I must not weep. 1490
Now, maidens, let us join
in praise of Artemis,
Artemis in her temple
across Chalcis strait,
where now in Aulis gulf,
and by the narrows,
wooden ships rage fiercely
in my name. 1495
O motherland Pelasgia,
Mycenae, my Mycenae
who fostered me . . .

CHORUS [singing]
  Do you call on Perseus' citadel 1500
  wrought by the hands of the Cyclopes?

IPHIGENIA
  . . . fostered me,
  a light to Greece.
  I do not refuse to die for you.

CHORUS
  Never will your glory pass away.

IPHIGENIA
  O dayspring 1505
  torch of Zeus

and glorious light!
To another world I go
out of this place
to dwell.
And now, and now,
beloved light,
farewell!

(*Exit Iphigenia to the side.*)

CHORUS [*still singing*]
O look at the girl who walks   1510
to the goddess' altar
that Troy may be brought low
and the Phrygians die.
Her hair in garlands of honor,
and flung upon her body the lustral waters,
she will go to the goddess' altar
which she will stain,
and her lovely body's neck,
with streams of flowing blood.   1515
Oh, your father's waters await you,°
the waters of purification;
and the Greek army too awaits you
for their sailing to Troy.   1520
But now all hail to the daughter of Zeus,
all hail to Artemis, goddess queen,
as for a prosperous fate!
Goddess,
you who take joy in human blood,
escort the armies of all the Greeks
to the land of Phrygia   1525
and to the citadel of treacherous Troy;°
there give to Greece and to her spearmen
a crown of victory.
And for the king,

Agamemnon,
O touch his head   1530
with a glory everlasting.

          (Exit the Chorus to the side, Clytemnestra into the tent.)

[For the transmitted ending of the play, which is probably spurious, see the Appendix.]

APPENDIX TO IPHIGENIA IN AULIS

This appendix provides the transmitted ending of the play, which is probably spurious.°

(Enter Second Messenger from the side.)

MESSENGER
O daughter of Tyndareus, Clytemnestra,
come outside the pavilion and receive
my message.

(Enter Clytemnestra from the tent.)

CLYTEMNESTRA
    Hearing your voice calling, I am here,
wretched, fearful, and in terror that you   1535
have come to add a new disaster
to my present grief.

MESSENGER
        It is about your child—
I must recount a thing of awe and wonder.

CLYTEMNESTRA
Then don't delay, but tell it as quickly
as you can.

MESSENGER
I shall, and everything, dear mistress,   1540
you shall learn clearly from the beginning
unless my whirling thoughts trip up my tongue.

When we came to Artemis' grove and to
the flowered meadow of Zeus' daughter,
leading your child to the mustering ground
of the Achaeans, then quickly the army 1545
of Argives assembled.
And when King Agamemnon saw his girl
walk into the grove for the sacrifice
he groaned bitterly, and turning his head
wept, drawing his robe across his eyes. 1550
But she, standing beside her father, spoke:
"O Father, I am here at your command—
willingly I give my body to be 1555
sacrificed for my country, for all Greece.
If it be the will of heaven, lead me
to the goddess' altar. May you all prosper:
win victory in this war and then return
to your fatherland. But let no Argive
touch me with his hand. Silent, unflinching,
I offer my neck to the knife." These words 1560
she spoke, and every man hearing her wondered
at the maid's courage and nobility.

Then Talthybius, standing in the midst,
according to his office spoke, proclaiming
a holy silence to the army,
and Calchas, the prophet, unsheathing 1565
with his hand the sharp knife, laid it
in the golden basket. Then he crowned
the head of the girl. And the son of Peleus,
taking the barley and the lustral waters,
ran round the goddess' altar and cried out:
"O child of Zeus, O slayer of wild beasts, 1570
you who turn your disk of shining light
through the night's shadows, receive this sacrifice
which we make to you—we the Achaean host
and the king Agamemnon—unblemished blood
from the neck of this fair girl. And grant

that unharmed now the fleet may sail;   1575
and grant this too, that we and our spears destroy
the battlements of Troy."
             Then Atreus' sons
and the whole army stood with eyes bent on
the earth. And the priest, taking the knife,
uttered his prayer, and scanned her neck to strike
his blow. Oh, then I stood with my head
bowed, and a great anguish smote my heart—   1580
but suddenly a miracle came to pass.
Clearly all heard the blow strike home—
but after, with no man knowing where or how,
the maiden had vanished from the earth.
Then the priest with a great voice cried aloud
and the whole army echoed him—this when
they saw the apparition which a god had sent   1585
but no man had foreknown. Though our eyes saw,
it was a sight incredible: a deer
panting its last lay there on the earth,
big to behold and fine indeed. The goddess'
altar freely ran with the creature's blood.
At this Calchas spoke and with joy one can   1590
believe: "O commanders of the allied
armies, you see this victim which the goddess
had laid upon the altar, a mountain hind?
Rather than the maid, this victim she receives
with joy. By this no noble blood   1595
stains her altar. Gladly she accepts
this offering and grants a fair voyage
for our attack on Troy. Let every sailor
then be glad, and go to the galleys,
for on this day we must leave the hollow   1600
bays of Aulis, and cross the Aegean sea."
      Then when the victim had been burned
wholly to cinder in Hephaestus' flame,
he prayed for the army's safe return.

After all this King Agamemnon sent me
to report to you and tell what fortune   1605
had come from heaven and what deathless glory
she has won for Greece. And I who saw
this thing, being present, report it now to you.
Clearly your child was swept away to heaven;
so give over grief and cease from anger
against your husband. No mortal can foreknow   1610
the ways of heaven. Those whom the gods love
they rescue. For think, this day beheld
your child die, and come alive again.

CHORUS LEADER

With what gladness I hear the messenger's
report! Your child he tells us is alive
and dwelling with the gods in heaven.

CLYTEMNESTRA [*singing*]

O child! What god has stolen you from me?   1615
How can I ever call to you? How know
that this is not a false story merely told
that I may stop my bitter grieving?

CHORUS LEADER

Behold King Agamemnon comes to us,
and the same story he will tell to you.   1620

(Enter Agamemnon from the side.)

AGAMEMNON

My lady, we can now be happy
in our daughter's destiny. Truly she
dwells now in fellowship with the gods.
Now must you take this little son of ours
and journey home. The army's eyes are on
the voyage. It will be long, long,
before my greeting comes to you again   1625

on the return from Troy. Meantime
may all go well with you!

CHORUS [*chanting*]
With joy, son of Atreus, sail on
to the Phrygian land,
with joy return,
bringing glorious spoils from Troy!

THE CYCLOPS

Translated by WILLIAM ARROWSMITH

THE CYCLOPS: INTRODUCTION

The Play: Date and Composition

The Cyclops is not a tragedy but a satyr-play. It is the only complete specimen of this genre to have survived. The satyr-play was a type of drama similar to tragedy in being based on heroic myth and employing many of the same stylistic features, but distinguished by having a chorus of half-human, half-horse followers of Dionysus—sileni or satyrs, played by the same Athenian citizens as had played the tragic choruses in the three preceding plays, but costumed now in baldheaded masks, horse tails, and erect phalluses. Furthermore, satyr-plays always end happily and tend to be shorter and simpler than tragedies, to be far more ribald in matters sexual and alcoholic, and to be somewhat looser formally and musically. Usually they are set in the countryside or some exotic land, and their plotlines often involve the defeat of an ogre or monster. Each playwright's dramatic tetralogy at the Great Dionysian Festival in Athens usually consisted of three tragedies followed by one satyr-play (but we are told, for example, that Euripides' tragedy *Alcestis* took the place of the satyr-play in his tetralogy of 438 BCE). A vivid and informative picture of a satyr chorus preparing to perform, along with Silenus, heroic actors, and a pipe player, can be found on the famous Pronomos Vase, painted in Athens around the end of the fifth century BCE. (Images of this vase are widely available in books and on the web.)

Although we can be certain that Euripides wrote *The Cyclops* for the annual competition at that festival, there is no way to determine its exact or even approximate date: no external evidence indicates when it was produced, and the metrical features that provide an approximate sequence for Euripides' tragedies do

not apply to the satyr-plays. Scholars have suggested dates rang-
ing from the beginning to the end of Euripides' career; some
have tried looking for allusions in the play to particular political
events or to other plays of known date, but such attempts have
not been convincing. So too, what the other three plays were in
Euripides' tetralogy of that year, and how they fared in the dramatic competition, are entirely unknown.

The Myth

The Cyclops is a comic dramatization of a celebrated episode from
book 9 of the Odyssey: on his voyage home from Troy, Odysseus
lands on an island inhabited by the fearsome, man-eating, primitive, one-eyed Cyclops Polyphemus. Odysseus and some of his
crew are trapped in the monster's cave and start to be devoured
two at a time. But Odysseus saves himself and his remaining men
by an ingenious stratagem: he gets Polyphemus drunk and blinds
the sleeping Cyclops with a smoldering stake. Odysseus has told
him that his name is "Nobody," so that when Polyphemus calls
for help from his fellow Cyclopes they laugh at him when he can
only tell them that "Nobody" has blinded him. In the end, Odysseus and his men escape from the cave by hiding under the fleecy
bellies of the Cyclops' sheep.

In spite of the evident differences in dramatic medium and
comic tone, Euripides' play follows his Homeric model fairly
closely, though he has eliminated the huge rock blocking the
doorway and Odysseus' use of the sheep to escape, substituting for
these a macabre game of blindman's buff as the enraged Cyclops
tries to catch the escaping Greeks. The most obvious difference,
of course, is the insertion, into the very center of this serious epic
story, of the lascivious, childish, musical, and cowardly satyrs and
their comically dipsomaniacal and duplicitous leader Silenus.

The result is a sophisticated hybrid genre, a kind of romance-
drama that mixes epic, comic, and pastoral elements so as to provoke laughter and amusement at both the lowest and the highest
literary levels.

The Cyclops has never been one of Euripides' most popular dramas. It survived antiquity only by the accident of being among the so-called "alphabetic plays," (see "Introduction to Euripides," p. 3); it is transmitted only by a single manuscript (and its copies) and it is not accompanied by ancient commentaries (scholia) explaining interpretive difficulties. Nor have any papyri bearing parts of its text ever been discovered. Its impact on the visual arts seems to have been very limited, though one striking late fifth-century BCE vase painting does survive from Lucania (south Italy), depicting Odysseus and his crew in the act of blinding Polyphemus while satyrs scurry about them—a scene presumably inspired by this play.

So too, in its influence on modern literature and art, *The Cyclops* has been greatly overshadowed by Homer's epic version. But Euripides' play was translated by Percy Bysshe Shelley (1819), and it is occasionally staged, with considerable success. As the sole surviving example of a complete satyr-play, it also receives its share of critical attention in accounts of the origins and history of Greek drama, although scholars are unsure just how typical it really is.

THE CYCLOPS

Characters   SILENUS, father of the satyrs
                CHORUS of satyrs
                ODYSSEUS
                CYCLOPS, named Polyphemus

Scene: *In front of a cave at the foot of Mount Etna.*

(Enter Silenus from the cave.)

SILENUS

           O Bromius,
thanks to you, my troubles are as many now
as in my youth when my body still was strong!
First I remember when Hera drove you mad
and you left your nurses, the mountain nymphs.
And then there was that war with the Giants: 5
there I stood, on your right, covering your flank
with my shield. And I hit Enceladus with my spear
square on the center of his shield and killed him.
Or wait: was that in a dream? No, by Zeus,
for I displayed the actual spoils to Bacchus.
And now I must bail against a wilder wave   10
of trouble. For when I heard that Hera
had urged Tyrrhenian pirates to sell you
as a slave abroad, I hoisted sail with my sons
to search for you. Right on the stern I stood,
the tiller in my hands, steering the ship.   15
And my boys strained at the oars, churning white

the green sea in our search for you, my king!
And then we had almost rounded Cape Malea
when an east wind cracked down and drove us here,
to rocky Etna, where the one-eyed sons   20
of the sea god, the murderous Cyclopes,
live in their desolate caves. One of them—
they call him Polyphemus—captured us
and made us slaves in his house. So now,
instead of dancing in the feasts of Bacchus,   25
we herd the flocks of this godless Cyclops.

     So now, far off on the mountain slopes, my sons,
young as they are, watch the youngling herd.
I am assigned to stay and fill the troughs
and clean these quarters and play the chef   30
for the godless dinners of this impious Cyclops.
And now I must sweep the cave with this iron rake—
these are my orders—to welcome back home
my absent master and his flock of sheep.   35
But I see my sons shepherding their sheep
this way.

> (Enter the Chorus of satyrs from the side, with
> their flock of sheep and attendant slaves.)

    What? How can you dance like that?
Do you think you're mustered at Bacchus' feast
and swaggering your sexy way with lyre music
to the halls of Althaea?   40

CHORUS [singing]   (To a ram.)

STROPHE

You there, with the fine pedigree
on both sides, dam and sire,
   why run for the rocks?
Haven't you here a quiet breeze,
   green grass for the grazing?   45
Look: the water from the brook
   swirls through your troughs

beside the cave
where your small lambs bleat.

Hey, come here! Now!
Won't you feed on the dewy hill?   50
Move, or I'll pelt you with stones!
In with you, horny-head, move along
into the fold of Shepherd Cyclops!

(To a ewe.)

Relieve your swollen teats!   55
Come, suckle your young whom you left
    all alone in the lamb pens!
Asleep all day, your newborn lambs
    bleat that they want you.
Leave your cropping at Etna's rocks,   60
    and come into the fold!

No Bacchus here! Not here the dance,
or the women whirling the thyrsus,
or the timbrels shaken,   65
where the springs of water rill up!°
Not here the bright drop of wine,
and no more at Nysa with nymphs
do I sing the song "Iacchus! Iacchus!"
to Aphrodite,   70
she that I used to fly after
along with the barefooted Bacchae!
Dear lord Bacchius, where do you run,°
unattended now, tossing your auburn hair?   75
For I, your servant, am a wretched slave,
tricked out in dirty goatskin   80
serving a one-eyed Cyclops,
and out of the way of your love.

SILENUS
    Be quiet, my sons. Quick, order the attendants
    to corral the flocks into the rock fold.

CHORUS LEADER
    Move along there.

                              (The slaves do as instructed.)

            But why this hurry, father?

SILENUS
    I see a Greek ship drawn up on the shore   85
    and oarsmen led by a captain coming
    toward our cave. They carry water pitchers
    and empty containers about their necks:
    they'll want supplies. Poor strangers, who are they?
    They can't know what this Polyphemus is like,   90
    coming to this inhospitable land
    and—bad luck!—to the Cyclops' man-eating jaws.
    But hush, so we can learn from where they've come
    to Sicily and to Mount Etna.   95

                (Enter Odysseus from the side with his men.)

ODYSSEUS
    Strangers, could you tell us where we might find
    running water? We have nothing to drink.
    Would some one of you like to sell some food
    to hungry sailors? What? Do I see right?
    We must have come to the city of Dionysus.
    These are satyrs I see around the cave.   100
    Let me greet the oldest among you first.

SILENUS
    Greeting, stranger. Who are you, and from where?

ODYSSEUS
    I am Odysseus of Ithaca, king of the Cephallenians.

SILENUS

I've heard of you: a glib sharper, Sisyphus' bastard.

ODYSSEUS

I am he. Keep your abuse to yourself.   105

SILENUS

From what port did you set sail for Sicily?

ODYSSEUS

We come from Troy and from the war there.

SILENUS

What? Couldn't you chart your passage home?

ODYSSEUS

I was driven here by wind and storm.

SILENUS

Too bad. I had the same misfortune.   110

ODYSSEUS

You too were driven here from your course unwilling?

SILENUS

We were chasing the pirates who captured Bacchus.

ODYSSEUS

What is this place? And who inhabits it?

SILENUS

This is Etna, the highest peak in Sicily.

ODYSSEUS

Where are the walls and the city towers?   115

SILENUS

This is no city. No man inhabits here.

ODYSSEUS

Who does inhabit it? Wild animals?

SILENUS

The Cyclopes. They live in caves, not houses.

ODYSSEUS

Who governs them? Or do the people rule?

SILENUS

They are savages. There is no government. 120

ODYSSEUS

How do they live? Do they till the fields?

SILENUS

Their whole diet is milk, and cheese, and the meat of sheep.

ODYSSEUS

Do they grow grapes and make the vine give wine?

SILENUS

No. And the land is sullen. There is no dance.

ODYSSEUS

Are they hospitable to strangers here? 125

SILENUS

Strangers, they say, make the tastiest meal.

ODYSSEUS

What? You say they feast on human flesh?

SILENUS

Here every visitor always gets devoured.

ODYSSEUS

Where is this Cyclops now? In the . . . house?

SILENUS

Gone hunting on Mount Etna with his hounds. 130

ODYSSEUS

You know what you can do so we can escape?

SILENUS

I don't know, Odysseus. But I'll do what I can.

ODYSSEUS

Then sell us some bread. We have none left.

SILENUS

There is nothing to eat, I said, except meat.

ODYSSEUS

Meat is good too, and it will stop our hunger. 135

SILENUS

We have some curdled cheese. And there's cow's milk.

ODYSSEUS

Bring them out. The buyer should see what he buys.

SILENUS

Tell me, how much gold will you pay down?

ODYSSEUS

In money, nothing. But I have some wine.

SILENUS

Delicious word! How long since I've heard it. 140

ODYSSEUS

Maron, son of the god, gave me this wine.

SILENUS

Not the same lad I once reared in these arms?

ODYSSEUS

The son of Bacchius himself, to be brief.

SILENUS

Where is the wine? On board ship? You have it?

ODYSSEUS

In this flask, old man. Look for yourself. 145

SILENUS

That? That wouldn't make one swallow for me.°

ODYSSEUS

No? For each swallow you take, the flask gives two.

SILENUS

A fountain among fountains, that! I like it.

ODYSSEUS

Will you have it unwatered to start with?

SILENUS

That's fair. The buyer should have a sample.   150

ODYSSEUS

I have a cup here to go with the flask.

SILENUS

Pour away. A drink will jog my memory.

ODYSSEUS

There you are.

SILENUS

            Mmmmmm. Gods, what a bouquet!

ODYSSEUS

Can you see it?

SILENUS

            No, by Zeus, but I can whiff it.

ODYSSEUS

Taste it now. Then you'll sing its praises.   155

SILENUS

Mmmmmmaa. A dance for Bacchus! La de da.

ODYSSEUS

Didn't that purl down your gullet sweetly?

SILENUS

Right down to the tips of my toenails.

ODYSSEUS

Besides the wine, we'll give you money. 160

SILENUS

Money be damned! Just pour out the wine.

ODYSSEUS

Then bring out your cheese, or a lamb.

SILENUS

Right away.
I don't give a hoot for any master.
I would go mad for one cup of that wine!
I'd give away the herds of all the Cyclopes. 165
Once I get drunk and happy, I'd go jump
in the sea off the Leucadian rock!
The man who doesn't like to drink is mad.
Why, when you're drunk, you stand up stiff down here

(Gestures.)

and then get yourself a fistful of breast 170
and browse on the soft field ready to your hands.
You dance, and good-bye to troubles. Well then,
why shouldn't I adore a drink like that
and tell that stupid Cyclops to get lost
with his eye in the middle of his ugly head?

(Exit into the cave.)

CHORUS LEADER

Listen, Odysseus, we'd like a word with you. 175

ODYSSEUS

By all means. We are all friends here.

CHORUS LEADER

Did you take Helen when you took Troy?

ODYSSEUS

We rooted out the whole race of Priam.

CHORUS LEADER

When you took that woman, did you all take turns
and bang her? She liked variety in guys,   180
the fickle slut! Why, the sight of a man
with embroidered pants and a golden chain
so fluttered her, she left Menelaus,
a fine little man. If only there were   185
no women in the world—except with me!

> (Enter Silenus from the cave, carrying baskets
> of cheese and leading some lambs.)

SILENUS

King Odysseus, here are some lambs for you,
the fat of the flock, and here, a good stock
of creamed cheeses. Take them and leave the cave   190
as fast as you can. But first give me a drink
of that blessed wine to seal our bargain.
Oh, help us! Here comes the Cyclops! What shall we do?

ODYSSEUS

We're finished now, old man. Where can we run?

SILENUS

Into the cave. You can hide in there.   195

ODYSSEUS

Are you mad? Run right into the trap?

SILENUS

No danger. The rocks are full of hiding places.

ODYSSEUS

Never. Why, Troy itself would groan aloud
if we ran from one man. Many's the time
I stood off ten thousand Phrygians with my shield.   200

If die we must, then we must die with honor.
But if we live, we live with our old glory!

(Enter the Cyclops from the side, with attendants.)

CYCLOPS

Here. Here. What's going on? What is this idleness?
Why this Bacchic hubbub? There's no Dionysus here,
no bronze clackers or rattlings of drums!   205
How are my newborn lambs in the cave?
Are they at the teat, nuzzling their mothers?
Are the wicker presses filled with fresh cheese?
Well? What do you say? Answer, or my club   210
will drub the tears out of you! Look up, not down.

CHORUS LEADER   *(To the Cyclops.)*

There. We're looking right up at Zeus himself.
I can see Orion and all the stars.

CYCLOPS

Is my dinner cooked and ready to eat?

CHORUS LEADER

Ready and waiting. You only need to swallow.   215

CYCLOPS

And are the vats filled up, brimming with milk?

CHORUS LEADER

You can swill a whole hogshead, if you like.

CYCLOPS

Cow's milk, or sheep's milk, or mixed?

CHORUS LEADER

Whatever you like. Just don't swallow me.

CYCLOPS

You least. I'd soon be dead if I had you   220
dancing your fancy moves inside my belly.

(He sees the Greeks standing near the cave.)

Hey! what's that crowd I see over by my cave?
Have pirates or thieves taken the country?
Look: lambs from my fold tied up with willow twigs!   225
And cheese-presses all around! And the Old Man
with his bald head swollen red with bruises!

SILENUS
Ohhh. I'm all on fire. They've beaten me up.

CYCLOPS
Who did? Who's been beating your head, old man?

SILENUS   *(Indicating the Greeks.)*
They did, Cyclops. I wouldn't let them rob you.   230

CYCLOPS
Didn't they know that I am a god?
Didn't they know my ancestors were gods?

SILENUS
I tried to tell them. But they went on robbing.
I tried to stop them from stealing your lambs
and eating your cheeses. What's more, they said
they would yoke you to a three-foot collar   235
and squeeze out your bowels through your one eye,
and scourge your backsides with a whip,
and then they were going to tie you up
and throw you on their ship and auction you
for hauling rocks or slaving at a mill.   240

CYCLOPS
Is that so?

(To a servant.)

Run and sharpen my cleavers.
Take a big bunch of firewood and light it.

(Exit a servant into the cave.)

I'll slaughter them right now and stuff my maw.
I'll give the carver their meat red-hot from the coals,   245
the other pieces boiled in the cauldron
and tender. I'm fed up with mountain food:
too many lions and stags and far too long
since I've had a good meal of man meat.

SILENUS

And quite right, master. A change in diet   250
is always pleasant. It's been a long time
since we've had visitors here at the cave.

ODYSSEUS

Cyclops, let your visitors have their say.
We came here to your cave from our ship
wanting to buy some food. This fellow here   255
sold us some lambs in exchange for wine—
all quite voluntary, no coercion.
There's not a healthy word in what he says;
the fact is he was caught peddling your goods.   260

SILENUS

I? Why, damn your soul.

ODYSSEUS

            Yes—if I'm lying.

SILENUS

I swear, Cyclops, by your father Poseidon,
by Triton the great, I swear by Nereus,
by Calypso and by Nereus' daughters,
by the holy waves and every species of fish,   265
I swear, dear master, lovely little Cyclops,
I did not try to sell your goods to strangers!
If I did, then let my dear children die for it.

CHORUS LEADER

And the same to you. With these very eyes
I saw you selling goods to the strangers.   270

And if I'm lying, then let my father
die for it. But don't do wrong to strangers.

CYCLOPS

You're lying. I would rather believe him

(Indicating Silenus.)

than Rhadamanthus himself. And I say
that he's right. But I want to question you.
Where have you sailed from, strangers? What's your country?   275
Tell me in what city you grew up.

ODYSSEUS

We are from Ithaca. After we sacked
the city of Troy, sea winds drove us here,
safe and sound, to your country, Cyclops.

CYCLOPS

Was it you who sacked Troy-on-Scamander   280
because that foul Helen was carried off?

ODYSSEUS

We did. Our terrible task is done.

CYCLOPS

You ought to die for shame: to go to war
with the Phrygians for a single woman!

ODYSSEUS

A god was responsible; don't blame mortals.   285
But we ask as free men, we implore you,
do not, O noble son of the sea god,
murder men who come to your cave as friends.
Do not profane your mouth by eating us.
        For it is we, my lord, who everywhere
in Hellas preserved your father Poseidon   290
in the tenure of his temples. Thanks to us,
Taenarus' sacred harbor is inviolate,
Cape Malea too with all its mountain hollows;

the peak of Sunium with its silver lodes
sacred to Athena, is still untouched;
and safe, the sanctuaries of Geraestus!   295
We did not betray Greece—perish the thought!°—
to Phrygians. And you have a share in this:
for this whole land, under volcanic Etna
in whose depths you live, is part of Hellas.

    In any case—and even if you disagree—
all men honor the rule that shipwrecked sailors   300
must be received and given clothes and presents.
Above all, they should not gorge your mouth and belly,
nor be spitted as men might spit an ox.
The land of Priam has exhausted Greece,
soaked up the blood of thousands killed in war: 305
wives made widows, old women and gray-haired men
without their sons. If you roast the rest
for your ungodly meal, where will people turn?
Change your mind, Cyclops! Forget your hunger!   310
Forget this sacrilege and do what is right.
Many have paid the price for base profits.

SILENUS

A word of advice, Cyclops. Eat every bit
of him. And if you chew on his tongue,
you'll become eloquent and very glib.   315

CYCLOPS

Money's the wise man's religion, little man.
The rest is mere bluff and purple patches.
I don't give a damn for my father's shrines
along the coast! Why did you think I would?
And I'm not afraid of Zeus's thunder;   320
in fact, I don't think Zeus is a stronger god
than I am. And anyway I don't care,
and I'll tell you why I don't care. When Zeus
pours down rain, I take shelter in this cave
and feast myself on roast veal or venison.   325

Then I stretch myself and wash down the meal,
flooding my belly with a vat of milk.
Then I strike it with my hand, louder than ever
Zeus can thunder. When the wind sweeps down
with snow from Thrace, I wrap myself in furs   330
and light up the fire. Then let it snow
for all I care! Whether it wants or not,
the earth must grow the grass that feeds my flocks.
And as for sacrifices, I make mine,
not to some other gods, but to the greatest   335
of all: me and my belly! To eat, to drink
from day to day, to have no worries—
that's the real Zeus for your man of sense!
As for those who embroider human life
with their little laws—damn the lot of them!   340
I shall go right on indulging myself—
by eating you. But, to be in the clear,
I'll be hospitable and give you fire
and my father's water°—plus a cauldron.
Once it starts to boil, it will clothe your flesh
better than these rags. So go inside   345
and gather round the altar to the god
of the cave, and wish me hearty eating.

ODYSSEUS

Gods! Have I escaped our hardships at Troy
and on the seas only to be cast up
and wrecked on the reef of this savage heart?
O Pallas, lady, daughter of Zeus, now   350
if ever, help me! Worse than war at Troy,
I have come to my danger's deepest place.
O Zeus, god of strangers, look down on me
from where you sit, throned among the bright stars!
If you do not look down upon me now,
you are no Zeus, but a nothing at all!   355

*(Exit the Cyclops and attendants into the cave, dragging
Odysseus and his men and followed by Silenus.)*

CHORUS [*singing*]

STROPHE

Open the vast O of your jaws, Cyclops!
Dinner is served: the limbs of your guests,
boiled, roasted, or broiled, ready for you
    to gnaw, rend, and chew
while you loll on your shaggy goatskin.   360

MESODE

Don't ask me to dinner. Stow that cargo
on your own. Let me keep clear of this cave,
well clear of the Cyclops of Etna,
    this loathsome glutton,   365
who gorges himself on the guts of his guests!

ANTISTROPHE

Savage! Stranger to mercy! A monster
who butchers his guests on his hearth,
who boils up their flesh and eats it,   370
    whose foul mouth munches
on human meat plucked from the sizzling coals!°

(Enter Odysseus from the cave.)

ODYSSEUS

Zeus, how can I say what I saw in that cave?   375
Unbelievable horrors, the kind of things
men hear about in myths, not in real life!

CHORUS LEADER

Has that godforsaken Cyclops butchered
your crew? Tell us what happened, Odysseus.

ODYSSEUS

He snatched up two of my men, the soundest
and plumpest. He weighed them in his hands.   380

CHORUS LEADER
How horrible! How could you stand to watch?

ODYSSEUS
First, after we had entered the cave,
he lit a fire and tossed down on the huge hearth
logs from a vast oak—you would have needed
three wagons merely to carry the load.   385
Then he pulled his pallet of pine needles
close to the fire. After he milked the cows,
he filled a hundred-gallon vat with milk.
By his side, he put an ivy-wood box,
about four feet in width and six feet deep.   390
Next he put a cauldron of brass to boil
on the fire, and beside it thorn-wood spits
whose points had been sharpened in the coals
and the rest trimmed down with an axe. There were°
bowls for catching blood, big as Etna,
and set flush against the blade of the axe.   395
Well, when this damned cook of Hades was ready,
he snatched up two of my men. With one blow
he slit the throat of one over the lip
of the brass cauldron.° Holding the other
by the heels, he slammed him against a rock   400
and bashed out his brains. Then he hacked away
the flesh with his terrible cleaver
and put the pieces to roast on the coals.
The leftovers he tossed in the pot to boil.
With the tears streaming down, I went up close   405
and waited on the Cyclops. The others,
their faces ashen, huddled up like birds
in the crannies of the rocks. Then he leaned back,
bloated with his awful meal on my men,
and let out a staggering belch.
                              Just then   410
some god sent me a marvelous idea!

I filled a cup and gave him Maron's wine
to drink. "Cyclops," I said, "son of the sea god,
see what a heavenly drink yield the grapes
of Greece, the gladness of Dionysus!"   415
Glutted with his dreadful meal, he took it
and drained it off at one gulp, then lifted
his hands in thanks: "You are the best of guests!
You have given me a noble drink to crown
a noble meal." When I saw how pleased he was,   420
I poured him another, knowing the wine
would quickly fuddle him and pay him back.
Then he started to sing. I poured one drink
after another and warmed his belly.
So there he is, inside, singing away   425
while my crew wails; you can hear the uproar.
I slipped out quietly. Now, if you agree,
I'd like to save myself and you as well.
So tell me, yes or no, whether you want
to escape this monster and live with the nymphs   430
in the halls of Bacchius. Your father in there
agrees, but he's weak and loves his liquor.
He's stuck to the cup as though it were glue,
and can't fly. But you are young, so follow me
and save yourselves; find again your old friend,   435
Dionysus, so different from this Cyclops!

CHORUS LEADER
My good friend, if only we might see that day
when we escape at last this godless Cyclops!

(Showing his phallus.)

This poor hose has been a bachelor°
a long time now. But we can't eat the Cyclops back!   440

ODYSSEUS
Listen to my plan for setting you free
and getting revenge upon this loathsome beast.

CHORUS LEADER

Tell on. I would rather hear tell of his death
than hear all the harps in Asia play.

ODYSSEUS

He is so delighted with Bacchus' drink   445
he wants to carouse with his relatives.

CHORUS LEADER

I see. You'll set an ambush in the woods
and kill him—or push him over a cliff.

ODYSSEUS

No, I had something more subtle in mind.

CHORUS LEADER

I've always heard that you are sly. What then?   450

ODYSSEUS

I hope to stop him from going on this spree
by saying he shouldn't give his wine away,
but keep it for himself and live in bliss.
Then, as soon as the wine puts him to sleep,
I'll take my sword and sharpen up the branch   455
of an olive tree I saw inside the cave.
I'll put it in the coals and when it's burnt,
I'll shove it home, dead in the Cyclops' eye,
and blind him. Just like a timber-fitter
whirling his auger around with a belt,   460
I'll screw the brand in his eye, round and round,
scorch out his eyeball and blind him for good.

CHORUS LEADER

Bravo! I'm for your plan with all my heart.   465

ODYSSEUS

And finally, my friends, I'll embark you
and your old father aboard my black ship
and sail full speed away from this place.

CHORUS LEADER

  May I lend a hand at this ritual?
  Help hold the pole when you put out his eye?   470
  This is one sacrifice I want to share.

ODYSSEUS

  You must. The brand is huge. You all must lift.

CHORUS LEADER

  I could shoulder a hundred wagonloads
  so long as Cyclops gets what he deserves!
  We'll smoke out his eye like a hornets' nest.   475

ODYSSEUS

  Be quiet now. You know my stratagem.
  When I give the word, obey your leaders.
  I refuse to save myself and leave my men
  trapped inside. I could, of course, escape:°
  here I am, outside. But I have no right   480
  to abandon my crew and save myself alone.

CHORUS [chanting]

  Who'll be first along the brand? Who next?
  We'll shove it square in the Cyclops' eye!
  We'll pulverize his sight.   485

                    (Singing is heard from within the cave.)

                        Quiet.
                              Shhhh.
  Here he comes, flat, off-key drunkard,
  reeling out of his home in the rock,   490
  braying some wretched tune. Ha!
  We'll give him lessons in carousing!
  A little while: then, perfect blindness!

            (Enter Polyphemus from the cave, accompanied by Silenus.)

  [*The Chorus continues to sing in this lyric interchange with the Cyclops,*
  who sings in reply]

Happy the man who cries "Euhoi!"   495
just itching to make merry,
for whom the wine keeps flowing,
whose arms are open to his friend!
Lucky man, upon whose bed there waits
the soft bloom of a lovely girl!   500
With gleaming hair, sweet with oil,
he cries: "Who'll open the door for me?"

CYCLOPS

STROPHE B

Mamama. Am I crammed with wine!
How I love the fun of a feast!
The hold of my little ship   505
is stuffed right up to the top deck!
This marvelous meal reminds me:
I should go carouse with my brothers
the Cyclopes, in the springtime.
Here, here, my friend, hand me the flask.   510

CHORUS

STROPHE C

O the flash of a handsome eye!
Handsome himself comes from his house,
Handsome the groom, Handsome the lover!°
A soft bride burns for this groom;   515
she burns in the cool of the cave!
And soon we shall wreathe his head
with a wreath of reddest flowers!

ODYSSEUS [*speaking*]

Listen, Cyclops. I've spent a lot of time
with this drink of Bacchus I gave you.   520

CYCLOPS [*speaking*]

Who is this Bacchus? Worshipped as a god?

ODYSSEUS

Best of all in blessing the lives of men.

CYCLOPS

At least he makes very tasty belching.

ODYSSEUS

That's the kind of god he is: hurts no one.

CYCLOPS

How can a god bear to live in a flask?   525

ODYSSEUS

Wherever you put him, he's quite content.

CYCLOPS

Gods shouldn't clothe themselves in animal skins.

ODYSSEUS

What matter, if you like him? Does the flask irk you?

CYCLOPS

I loathe the flask. The wine is what I like.

ODYSSEUS

Then you should stay here and enjoy yourself.   530

CYCLOPS

Shouldn't I share the wine with my brothers?

ODYSSEUS

Keep it to yourself; you'll be more esteemed.

CYCLOPS

But I'd be more useful if I shared it.

ODYSSEUS

Yes, but carousing often ends in fights.

CYCLOPS

I'm so drunk nothing could hurt me now.   535

ODYSSEUS

My dear man, drunkards ought to stay at home.

CYCLOPS

But the man's a fool who drinks by himself.

ODYSSEUS

It's the wise man who stays home when he's drunk.

CYCLOPS

What should we do, Silenus? Should I stay home?

SILENUS

I would. Why do we want more drinkers, Cyclops?   540

CYCLOPS

Anyway, the ground is soft with flowers.

SILENUS

There's nothing like a drink when the sun is hot.
Lie down there; stretch yourself out on the ground.

> *(The Cyclops does as instructed, and Silenus
> puts the wine bowl behind his back.)*

CYCLOPS

There. Why did you put the bowl behind my back?   545

SILENUS

Someone might tip it over.

CYCLOPS

                                   You wanted
to steal a drink. Put it in the middle.
You there, stranger, tell me what your name is.

ODYSSEUS

Nobody is my name. But how will you reward me?

CYCLOPS

I will eat you the last of all your crew.   550

SILENUS

That's a fine gift to give your guest, Cyclops.

(He furtively drinks some wine.)

CYCLOPS

What are you doing? Drinking on the sly?

SILENUS

The wine kissed me—for my beautiful eyes.

CYCLOPS

Watch out. You love the wine; it doesn't love you.

SILENUS

Yes, by Zeus, it has a passion for my good looks.   555

CYCLOPS

Here, pour me a cupful, give it to me.

SILENUS

How is the mixture? Let me taste and see.

(He takes a quick drink.)

CYCLOPS

Damnation! give it here.

SILENUS

                         By Zeus, not before
I see you crowned—

(He gives the Cyclops a wreath of flowers.)

                      and have another drink.

(He empties the cup.)

CYCLOPS

This wine-pourer is a cheat!   560

SILENUS

                         Not at all.

The wine's so good it slides down by itself.
Now wipe yourself off before you drink again.

CYCLOPS

There. My mouth is clean and so is my beard.

SILENUS

Then crook your arm—gracefully now—and drink,
just as you see me drink—and now you don't.

(He empties the cup.)

CYCLOPS

Here! What are you doing?   565

SILENUS

                    Guzzling sweetly.

CYCLOPS   *(Snatching away the cup and handing it to Odysseus.)*
Here, stranger. Take the flask and pour for me.

ODYSSEUS

At least the wine feels at home in my hand.

CYCLOPS

Come on, pour!

ODYSSEUS

                    I am pouring. Relax, friend.

CYCLOPS

Relax? That's not so easy when you're drunk.

ODYSSEUS

There, take it up and drink down every drop,   570
and don't say die until the wine is gone.

CYCLOPS

Mama. What a wizard the vine must be!

ODYSSEUS

If you drench yourself on a full stomach

and swill your belly, you'll sleep like a log.
Leave a drop, and Bacchus will shrivel you up. 575

CYCLOPS (*He takes a long drink.*)
Whoosh! I can scarcely swim out of this flood.
Pure pleasure! Ohhh. Earth and sky whirling around,
all jumbled up together! Look: I can see
the throne of Zeus and the holy glory 580
of the gods.
        Couldn't I make love to them?
Those Graces tempt me! But my Ganymede here

(*He grabs Silenus.*)

is good enough for me. With him I'll sleep
better than with the Graces.° Yes, I will!
And anyway, I prefer boys to girls.

SILENUS
Am I Zeus' little Ganymede, Cyclops? 585

CYCLOPS
You are, by Zeus! The boy I'm grabbing from Dardanus!

SILENUS
I'm done for, children. Ghastly things await me.

CYCLOPS
Sneer at your lover, do you, because he's drunk?

SILENUS
It's a bitter wine I'll have to drink now.

(*Exit the Cyclops into the cave, dragging Silenus.*)

ODYSSEUS
To work, you noble sons of Dionysus! 590
Our man's inside the cave. In a short while
his belly will heave its foul meal of flesh.
The firebrand has begun to smoke inside.

We prepared it for just this: to burn out
the Cyclops' eye. Now you must act like men.   595

CHORUS LEADER

Our will is made of unbreakable rock.
But hurry inside before it happens
to my father. All is ready out here.

ODYSSEUS

O Hephaestus, ruler over Etna,
free yourself from this vile neighbor of yours!
Sear out his bright eye at one blow! O Sleep,   600
child of black Night, leap with all your might
on this god-detested beast! And do not,
after our glorious trials at Troy,
betray Odysseus and his crew to death
from a man who cares for neither man nor god.   605
If you do, we will make a goddess of Chance,
and count her higher than all the other gods!

(Exit Odysseus into the cave.)

CHORUS [*singing*]

Grim tongs shall clutch by the throat
this beast who bolts down his guests.
Fire shall quench the fire of his eye.   610
The brand, big as a tree, already waits,
waits in the coals.   615
          On, wine, to your work!
Rip out the eye of this raving Cyclops!
Make him regret the day he drank you!
I want with all my soul to see
Bacchus, the god who loves the ivy,   620
and to leave the Cyclops' savage cage!
Shall I ever see that day?

(Enter Odysseus from the cave.)

ODYSSEUS [*speaking*]
> Quiet, you animals! By the gods, be quiet!
> Hold your tongues. I don't want a man of you
> to blink or clear his throat or even breathe. 625
> If we wake up that scourge of evil,
> we won't be able to sear out his eye.

CHORUS LEADER
> We *are* quiet. Our mouths are locked up tight.

ODYSSEUS
> To work then. And grab the brand with both hands 630
> when you enter the cave. The point is red-hot.

CHORUS LEADER
> You should tell us our stations. Who'll be first
> on the blazing pole? And then we can all
> take our fair part in what fortune assigns.

ONE CHORUS MEMBER
> Where we stand, over here by the entrance, 635
> we're too far away to reach his eye.

ANOTHER CHORUS MEMBER
> And just this minute we've gone lame.

FIRST CHORUS MEMBER
> And we have too. While we were standing here
> we sprained our ankles, I don't know how.

ODYSSEUS
> Sprained your ankles, standing still? 640

SECOND CHORUS MEMBER
>   And my eyes
> are full of dust and ashes from somewhere.

ODYSSEUS
> What worthless cowards! There's no help from you.

CHORUS LEADER

And just because I pity my back and spine
and don't want to have my teeth knocked out,
I'm a coward, am I? But I can sing   645
a fine Orphic spell that will make the brand
fly of its own accord into the skull
of this one-eyed whelp of Earth and scorch him up.

ODYSSEUS

I knew from the first what sort you were,
but now I know it better. So I guess
I'll have to use my own men. If you're too weak   650
to lend a hand, at least cheer them along
and put some heart in them with cries and chants.

(Exit Odysseus into the cave.)

CHORUS LEADER

We'll do that—and leave it to others to run the risks.
We'll scorch the Cyclops—but only with our singing.   655

CHORUS [*singing*]

Go! Go! As hard as you can!
Push! Thrust! Faster! Burn off
the eyebrow of the guest-eater!
Smoke him out, burn him out,
the shepherd of Etna!   660
Twist it! Turn! Careful:
he is hurt and desperate.

CYCLOPS   *(From within.)*

Owwooooo! My eye is scorched to ashes!   665

CHORUS LEADER [*speaking*]

Oh song of songs! Sing it for me, Cyclops!

CYCLOPS   *(From within.)*

Owwoo! They've murdered me! I'm finished!
But you won't escape this cave to enjoy

your triumph, you contemptible nothings.
I'll stand at the entrance and block it—so.

*(The Cyclops appears at the entrance of the
cave, his face streaming with blood.)*

CHORUS LEADER
What's the matter, Cyclops?

CYCLOPS
       I'm done for.

CHORUS LEADER
You look terrible.

CYCLOPS
       I feel terrible.   670

CHORUS LEADER
Did you get so drunk you fell in the fire?

CYCLOPS
Nobody wounded me.

CHORUS LEADER
       Then you're not hurt.

CYCLOPS
Nobody blinded me.

CHORUS LEADER
       Then you're not blind.

CYCLOPS
Blind as you.°

CHORUS LEADER
       How could nobody make you blind?

CYCLOPS
You mock me. Where is Nobody?   675

CHORUS LEADER
       Nowhere.

CYCLOPS
   It's the stranger I mean, you fool, the one
   who pumped me full of wine and did me in.

CHORUS LEADER
   Wine is tricky; very hard to wrestle with.

CYCLOPS
   By the gods, have they escaped or are they inside?

CHORUS LEADER
   There they are, standing quiet over there,   680
   under cover of the rock.

CYCLOPS
                     On which side?

CHORUS LEADER
   On your right.

   (The Cyclops leaves the entrance, and the Greeks steal out of the cave.)

CYCLOPS
                     Where?

CHORUS LEADER
                     Over against the rock.
   Do you have them?

CYCLOPS   *(Running into a rock.)*
                     Ouf! Trouble on trouble.
   I've split my head.

CHORUS LEADER
                     And now they've escaped you.

CYCLOPS
   This way, did you say?

CHORUS LEADER
                     No, the other way.

CYCLOPS

Which way?

CHORUS LEADER

     Turn around. There. On your left.   685

CYCLOPS

You're laughing at me in my misery.

CHORUS LEADER

Not now. There he is in front of you.

CYCLOPS

Where are you, demon?

ODYSSEUS

     Out of your reach,
Looking after the safety of Odysseus.   690

CYCLOPS

What? A new name? Have you changed your name?

ODYSSEUS

Odysseus: the name my father gave me.
You have had to pay for your unholy meal.
I would have done wrong to have fired Troy
but not revenge the murder of my men.   695

CYCLOPS

Ah! The old oracle has been fulfilled.
It said that after you had come from Troy,
you would blind me. But you would pay for this,
it said, and wander the seas for many years.   700

ODYSSEUS

Much I care! What's done is done. As for me,
I'm off to the shore where I'll launch my ship
on the Sicilian sea and sail for home.

       (Exit Odysseus and his men to the side.)

CYCLOPS

Not yet. I'll rip a boulder from this cliff
and crush you and all your crew beneath it.   705
Blind I may be, but I'll reach the mountaintop
soon enough through the tunnel in the cave.

(Exit into the cave.)

CHORUS

And we'll enlist in the crew of Odysseus.
From now on our orders come from Bacchius.

RHESUS

Translated by RICHMOND LATTIMORE

RHESUS: INTRODUCTION

The Play: Date and Composition

The date and even the authorship of *Rhesus* are unknown. It is transmitted among the works of Euripides. But according to a hypothesis (a summary) of the play, already some ancient scholars thought it was spurious; they argued that it seemed more Sophoclean than Euripidean (perhaps what they had in mind is that there are almost no female characters in the play). Others pointed out, however, that a play with this title by Euripides was included in the records of the competitions at the Greater Dionysian Festival in Athens, and that the curiosity about astronomical matters it manifests (for example, lines 528-31) was typical of Euripides. The play's authorship is still debated by modern scholars, especially since the eighteenth century. Those who deny its attribution to Euripides do so on linguistic, metrical, stylistic, and dramaturgical grounds, while those who defend it usually think the play must have been written early in Euripides' career. Although the question will probably never be resolved definitively, the great majority of contemporary scholars consider that *Rhesus* was written not by Euripides but by some unknown tragedian, most probably sometime in the fourth century BCE, and that it entered his collected works by mistake in place of a genuine *Rhesus* written by Euripides but which had been lost.

The Myth

Rhesus is the only surviving Greek tragedy whose plot is taken directly from one of the two great Homeric epics. Its story coincides with an episode from book 10 of the *Iliad*. At a particularly difficult moment for the Greeks, when Achilles has withdrawn from battle in anger at Agamemnon and the Trojans are gaining the upper hand, both sides send out spies during the night to reconnoiter the enemy. The Greek spies, Odysseus and Diomedes, capture and kill the Trojan one and return to their camp after they also kill Rhesus, king of the Thracian allies of the Trojans, slaughter a number of his men, and steal his marvelous horses.

Despite its title, *Rhesus* is centered from beginning to end upon the figure of Hector, whom it sets into a series of stark contrasts with all the other characters and with the chorus. The play follows the Homeric story fairly closely but views the events from the Trojan perspective rather than from the Greek one. Moreover, it elaborates upon some aspects that are absent or only hinted at in the epic version (for example, the disastrous consequences for the Greeks if Rhesus should survive to the next day) and involves many changes in tone and characterization (Hector here is far stupider, and Rhesus much more bellicose, than in Homer). It is possible that its author drew upon other, now lost sources besides the *Iliad*.

The play begins with the Trojan sentries waking Hector to warn him that the Greeks have lit watch fires. Aeneas persuades him not to attack the enemy at once, but to send a spy instead to find out what they are up to, and Dolon volunteers for the mission. Then Rhesus arrives with his Thracian army, and Hector and he discuss what to do before Hector leads him to the encampment where he is to spend the night. Odysseus and Diomedes enter cautiously: they have captured and killed Dolon, and Athena directs them to kill Rhesus, after which they escape. Rhesus' wounded charioteer recounts his master's death; and finally one of the Muses, the mother of Rhesus, appears, bearing her son's corpse and lamenting his death.

The play as transmitted begins, uniquely among Greek tragedies, with a lively scene of dialogue chanted in anapests between the chorus as it enters and Hector. One would expect it to begin instead with a prologue spoken by characters; and in fact the hypothesis mentioned above indicates that two such prologues were extant in antiquity. Of one it provides only the first line, which indicates the hour of the night by reference to celestial phenomena; of the other—which the author of this hypothesis describes as being very prosaic, not worthy of Euripides, and perhaps composed by some actors—it gives eleven lines that are addressed by Hera to Athena asking her help in destroying Troy. (Both of these prologue beginnings can be found in the first textual note to this play in this volume.) Scholars disagree about how to explain this odd situation. Some have suggested that the single line came from some completely different play and that the longer passage was the original beginning of this one, subsequently lost in direct transmission. But other explanations seem no less probable. Perhaps the one line belonged to the original version of the prologue of this very play, but that opening was lost at some point; later the longer one was written as part of a new opening in order to provide at least some kind of prologue, but then it too was not transmitted together with the rest of the play. The question remains open.

Transmission and Reception

Rhesus has never been one of the most popular plays in the Euripidean corpus. But some quotations and allusions from later ancient writers, and two papyri that preserve parts of its hypothesis or text, suggest that it did enjoy at least a limited readership.

Furthermore, it was selected to be one of the ten plays by Euripides that were most widely diffused during ancient and medieval times; perhaps this choice was influenced by the play's use of a Homeric story. As a result, it is transmitted by about five primary manuscripts and their copies, and it is equipped with some ancient commentaries (scholia) that explain various kinds of interpretive difficulties. The play seems to have left its trace on several south Italic vases of the mid-fourth century BCE that show the death of Rhesus. But its influence on modern literature and art has been negligible, and only rarely has it been translated, adapted, or performed.

RHESUS

Characters CHORUS of Trojan guards
HECTOR, a Trojan prince
AENEAS, a Trojan chieftain
DOLON, a Trojan soldier
SHEPHERD
RHESUS, king of the Thracians
ODYSSEUS, a Greek chieftain
DIOMEDES, a Greek chieftain
ATHENA
ALEXANDER (Paris), brother of Hector
CHARIOTEER OF RHESUS
THE MUSE, mother of Rhesus

*The tent of Hector in the Trojan camp on the plain between the city
and the shore. It is late at night.°*

> *(Enter from the side, in haste, the Chorus of Trojan
> guards, headed by an officer [the Chorus Leader].)*

CHORUS LEADER° [*chanting*]
   *Go find where Hector is sleeping. Ho there,
   is any of the king's bodyguard awake,
   or his armor-bearers?
   There is a new message he must hear
   from those who keep this quarter of the night's   5
   guard duty for the entire army:*
   "*Sit up, or lean your head on your arm;
   unclose your lids. Open your keen eyes.*

Rise now from the piled leaves of your bed,
Hector. A report. You must hear it."   10

                              (Enter Hector from inside the tent.)

HECTOR [chanting]
Who speaks? Enemy or friend? What is
the watchword? Speak.
Who comes here out of the night to find
where I sleep? Declare.

CHORUS LEADER
Sentries of the army.

HECTOR
                              What troubles you so?   15

CHORUS LEADER
Never fear.

HECTOR
                              Not I.°
What is it? A night raid?

CHORUS LEADER
                              No, not that.

HECTOR
                              Then why
have you left your post to come here and waken
the camp, unless we must form by night?
Do you realize that the Argive spears   20
are there, close by
where we sleep this night in our armor?

CHORUS [singing]
                              STROPHE
Arm, arm, Hector, and run to where
the allied forces lie sleeping.
Wake them, tell them to take their spears in their hands.   25
Send true men to run to your company;

have the curb chains put on the horses.
Someone go to Panthoüs' son
or Europa's, lord of the Lycian men. Who will?
Where are those who are in charge
of sacrifices? 30
Or the light-armed captains?
Where are the Phrygian archers?
Archers! Have your hornbows strung, quickly.

HECTOR [still chanting]

What you report seems partly alarm,
partly to be comfort. All is confusion. 35
What is this? Has the whiplash of Cronian Pan
struck you to shivering panic?° Speak, say,
what are you reporting? You have talked a great deal
without telling me one thing clearly. 40

CHORUS [singing]

ANTISTROPHE

The Argive army has lit its fires,
Hector, all through the darkness.
The positions of their ships are clear in the firelight.
But all their army has gathered in darkness
by Agamemnon's shelter, noisily. 45
They must wish to consult, to take
counsel, since never before was this sea-borne army
so utterly frightened. Therefore
I, to forestall anything that may happen,
came to report it, so that 50
you will not say I failed to do my duty.

HECTOR [now speaking]

Good. You are timely, though you come to us in alarm.
I see these people mean to row away by night,
quietly, when I cannot see them, and make good
their flight. I know exactly what their night fires mean. 55
O God, you robbed me, robbed the lion of his spoil.

All prospered, till you halted me before I swept
the Argive army to destruction with this spear.
For if the flaring lanterns of the sun had not
shut down against us, I would never have stayed my spear   60
in its fortune, until I had fired their ships, and made my way
through their camp, killing Achaeans with this murderous
    hand.
I myself was all ready to keep up the fight,
to use the darkness and the powerful force of god.
But the diviners, these educated men who know   65
the mind of heaven, persuaded me to wait for day—
and *then* to leave not one Greek alive on land.
But will they wait to be carefully slaughtered? No,
not they. The runaway slave is a great man by night.
Come, then. We must pass the order to our men, at once.   70
Have them wake and put on the armor that lies by.
So the Achaean, even while he jumps for his ship,
shall be stabbed in the back and drench the ladderways
with blood. And the survivors can be caught, and tied,
and learn to work the wheat fields in our land of Troy.   75

CHORUS LEADER [*now speaking*]
Too quick, Hector. You act before you understand.
We are not certain yet that they are running away.

HECTOR
For what cause did the Argives light their fires?

CHORUS LEADER
I do not know. I am suspicious of the whole matter.

HECTOR
If you fear this, you would be afraid of anything.   80

CHORUS LEADER
The enemy never lit fires like this before.

HECTOR
They never fled in such an awful rout before.

CHORUS LEADER

Yes. It was your work. Now consider what comes next.

HECTOR

There is only one order to give: arm and fight the enemy.

(Enter Aeneas from the side.)

CHORUS LEADER

Here comes Aeneas in great haste   85
of foot, as one who has news for his friends to hear.

AENEAS

Hector, why has the night guard of the camp come here
to where you were quartered? Is it panic? Here is talk
going on at night, and all the army is disturbed.

HECTOR

On with your armor quick, Aeneas.   90

AENEAS

                    Yes? What for?
Has someone come in to report the enemy
have made a surprise attack upon us in the dark?

HECTOR

No, no, they are withdrawing. They are boarding their ships.

AENEAS

And what good reason do you have to believe this?

HECTOR

Their watch fires are illuminating all the night,   95
and I believe they will not wait until the dawn
but burn them so that by their light they can escape
on their well-benched ships, to leave this country and go
    home.

AENEAS

What will you do about this, then? Why are you armed?

HECTOR

To fall upon them as they flee and board their ships,   100

to charge with our spears against them, and hit hard.
It would be shame, and more than shame, sheer cowardice,
to let them, when they did us so much harm, escape
without a fight, when a god has given them to our hands.

AENEAS
I wish you could make plans as well as you can fight.   105
But so it is: the same man cannot well be skilled
in everything; each has his special excellence,
and yours is fighting, and it is for others to make good plans,
not you. You heard how the Achaeans had lit their fires
and hope roused you to wish to lead the army on   110
across their deep moats in the time of night. Yet see,
suppose you do cross over the ditch, despite its depth,
and meet an enemy not withdrawing from our coast
as you think, but standing with spears faced to your attack—
you will have no free way to escape if they defeat you.   115
How will a beaten army cross the palisades?
How will your charioteers drive over the embankments
without smashing the axles of their chariots?
Then, even if you win, they have Achilles in reserve.
He will not sit by while you fire their ships; he will   120
not let you prey on the Achaeans, as you hope.
The man is hot, and he has massive strength of hand.
No, better, let us hold our army out of the way
of hard strokes; let them sleep at peace beside their shields;
but send one volunteer to scout the enemy.   125
So I think best. Then, if they really are in flight,
we can advance in force upon the Argive host.
But if this burning of their fires leads to some trick,
our scout will inform us what they are doing.
Then take our measures. This, my lord, is what I urge.   130

CHORUS [*singing*]

STROPHE

This is what I think best. Change your mind and accept it.
I do not like it when the general uses power that is

unsure. What could be better
than that a swift-paced man should go to spy on their ships,
from close, and see what it means   135
when our enemies have fires burning where their prows are
    beached?

HECTOR

You win, Aeneas, since this is approved by all.
Go, quiet our allies, let them sleep, since the whole army
might well be restless, hearing how we consult at night.
I will send a man to spy upon the enemy,   140
and if we find out that there is some stratagem,
you shall hear all, being near by, and be called to plan
with us; but if it is flight and they are casting off,
be ready for action when you hear the trumpet speak;
because I will not wait for you; I shall be there   145
among the Argives and their vessels, now, tonight.

AENEAS

Send him with all speed. Now your plan is sound. And if
the need comes for it, I will be as bold as you.

(Exit Aeneas to the side.)

HECTOR

Is there a Trojan, then, in earshot of my words,
who volunteers to spy upon the Argive ships?   150
Who is there who would have his country in his debt?
Who speaks? I cannot, by myself, do everything
that must be done to help our city and our friends.

(Enter Dolon from the side.)

DOLON

I will do it. For my country I undertake this cast
of hazard. I will go and scout the Argive ships   155
and listen to everything they plan to do and bring
word back. On such conditions I accept the task.

HECTOR

You are well named, my crafty Dolon, and you love
your city well. Your father's house was bright in name
before. Now you have made it twice as bright.   160

DOLON

It is good to work and fight, but when I do, it also
is good to be rewarded. For in every work
a reward added makes the pleasure twice as great.

HECTOR

True. I will not deny that what you say is fair.
Name your price. Anything except my royal power.   165

DOLON

I do not want your royal power, nor to rule a city.

HECTOR

Marry a daughter of Priam. Be my brother-in-law.

DOLON

I think it best not to marry above my station.

HECTOR

I have gold to give, if that is what you will be asking.

DOLON

We have it at home. We do not lack for anything.   170

HECTOR

What would you have out of the treasures of Ilium?

DOLON

Nothing. Catch the Achaeans, and then grant my gift.

HECTOR

I shall. But do not ask for the leaders of their fleet.

DOLON

Kill them. I will not ask for Menelaus' life.

HECTOR

It is not the son of Oileus you are asking me for?   175

DOLON

Those well-bred hands would never work well in the fields.

HECTOR

Is there any Achaean you would have alive, for ransom?

DOLON

I told you before. We have gold aplenty in our house.

HECTOR

Well, you shall come and take your own pick from the spoils.

DOLON

Take them, and nail them on the houses of the gods.   180

HECTOR

What prize greater than such things can you ask me for?

DOLON

The horses of Achilles.
                    Since I risk my life
on dice the gods throw, it must be for a high stake.

HECTOR

Ah. You are my rival, for I love those horses too.
They are immortal, born of an immortal strain,   185
who bear the fighting son of Peleus. The king
of the sea, Poseidon, broke them once and tamed them and
    gave
them to Peleus, so the story goes. Yet I have raised
your hopes, and I will not be false. I give you them:
Achilles' horses, a great possession for your house.   190

DOLON

I thank you. Thus my courage shall have a reward
that will outshine all others in the land of Troy.
But you should not be jealous. There is much besides
for you, our best and greatest, to take glory in.

CHORUS [singing]

ANTISTROPHE

High is the venture, high are the honors you hope to capture.   195

Blessed will your name be called if you win. For here
is glorious work to be done.
It would have been bold to marry into the house of our kings.
May the gods grant that Justice's eyes be on you,
as men now grant that all you deserve shall be yours.   200

DOLON

I am ready, once I have gone inside my house
and put upon my body the necessary gear.
From there, I shall take my way against the Argive ships.

CHORUS LEADER

What costume will you wear in place of what you have on?

DOLON

One suited to my venture and my stealthy way.   205

CHORUS LEADER

Some cleverness is to be learned from the clever man.
Tell me then, how do you mean to have your body arrayed?

DOLON

I shall put a wolfskin upon my back, fitted
so that the grinning jaws of the beast are on my head,
then, with the forepaws on my hands and the hind feet   210
upon my legs, shall imitate the four-foot tread
of the wolf, to puzzle the enemy who track me there
beside the ditch and by the bows of the beached ships.
Then when I reach the lonely stretch where no one is
I shall go upright. Thus my strategy is planned.   215

CHORUS LEADER

May Hermes, son of Maia, bring you there and bring
you back, since Hermes is the friend of slippery men.
You know your business. All you need now is good luck.

DOLON

I shall come safely back, but kill Odysseus first
and bring his head to you, to give you solid grounds   220

for saying Dolon won through to the Argive ships.
Or maybe Diomedes—but my hand will not
be bloodless when, before the day breaks, I come home.

(Exit to the side.)

CHORUS [*singing*]

STROPHE A

Lord of Thymbraeum, lord of Delos, who walk
in the holy Lycian shrine,   225
Apollo, O son of Zeus, come with your bow
armed, come in the night,
lead, preserve, and guide on his way this man
of battles, lend your strength to Dardanus' children,   230
O power complete, who long ago
founded the walls of Troy.

ANTISTROPHE A

Grant that he reach their shipsteads and come to spy
on the spread army of Greece
and turn and make his way back to the house of his father
and the sacred hearth, in Troy;   235
and grant, some day, he may mount the Phthian horse-chariot,
after our chief has smashed the war strength of Achaea,
and win the gift the sea god gave   240
once to Peleus, son of Aeacus.

STROPHE B

Yes, for he alone dared go down to spy on their ships
for our land and people. I admire
his courage; for indeed few   245
are found brave when the city
is a ship riding a hard
storm on the open
water. There is still manhood alive in Phrygia   250
and valor left still in her spears.
What Mysian is there who holds
scorn that I fight beside him?

ANTISTROPHE B

Who shall that man of Achaea be whom our stalking killer
will spear among the shelters as he goes   255
on fours in the pace of a lurking
beast? May it be Menelaus!
Or may he kill Agamemnon
and bring the head back
for Helen to lament, that evil brother of hers   260
by marriage. For it was he
who led the thousand ships
and the army here against Troy.

(Enter a Trojan Shepherd from the side.)

SHEPHERD

My lord, I hope I can always bring my masters news
as good as what I bring you now, for you to hear.   265

HECTOR

What crude creatures these yokels are. They have no sense.
You think it fitting to report about the flocks
to the armed nobility? You have no business here.
Do you not know where my house is, or my father's throne?
Go there for your announcement that the sheep are well.   270

SHEPHERD

We herdsmen are crude creatures, I will not say no.
Nevertheless, I am bringing good news for you.

HECTOR

Will you stop trying to tell me about what goes on
in the farmyard? We have spears and fighting on our hands.

SHEPHERD

But it is just such matters I report to you.   275
There is a man, with strength of thousands at his back,
who comes to fight for our country at your side.

HECTOR

Where are the native plains that he has emptied of men?

SHEPHERD

Thrace; and his father is called Strymon.

HECTOR

Do you mean
that Rhesus has set foot on Trojan soil?   280

SHEPHERD

You have it. So saved me half of what I had to say.

HECTOR

How did he lose the carriage road on the broad plains
to wander through the herds on Ida's mountainside?

SHEPHERD

I do not know exactly. I can guess at it.
It is no small thing to bring an army through the night   285
when you know the plain is full of enemies in arms.
We countrymen, who live where Ida runs to rock,
and plant our hearth on the bare ground, took alarm, as he
came through the oak wood with its animals in the night.
For this army of the Thracians streamed along   290
with great clamor, and we, terror-stricken, ran away
to the high pastures, fearing some Argives had come
on a plundering expedition and to rob your folds.
But then our ears made out their language; it was not
anything Greek, and now we were no more afraid.   295
I went and stood before the pathway of their scouts,
hailed them, and questioned them aloud in Thracian speech:
"Who rides as general here, and of what father called
comes he in arms to fight by Priam's citadel?"
Then, having heard answers to all I wished to know,   300
I stood and watched. There I saw Rhesus like a god
upright behind his horses in the Thracian car.
The golden balance of a yoke enclosed the necks
of his young horses, and these were whiter than snow.
The buckler on his shoulders glowed with beaten plates   305
of gold, and as upon a goddess' aegis, the bronze

face of a Gorgon on the horses' frontlet shields
glared, and with bells beat out a clashing sound of fear.
You could not reckon on an abacus the count
of all their army, so innumerable did it seem,   310
horsemen in numbers, numerous squads of buckler men,
many archers with their slender arrows, and, besides,
the light troops, in their Thracian costume, followed with
    them.
Such is the man who comes to fight for Troy. Neither
by flight, nor yet by standing to him with the spear,   315
will Peleus' son Achilles find escape from death.

CHORUS LEADER
When the gods change and stand behind the citizens,
a depressed fortune climbs uphill, and wins success.

HECTOR
Now that my spear is fortunate, and Zeus is on
our side, I shall be finding that I have many friends.   320
We can do without them. We want none who did not fight
our perils, past now, when the driving god of war
blew big upon our city's ship and wrecked our sails.
Rhesus has shown what kind of friend he is to Troy.
He is here for the feasting, but he was not here   325
with spear in hand to help the huntsmen catch the game.

CHORUS LEADER
Your grievance and complaint of friends is just. And yet,
accept those who, of their free will, will fight for us.

HECTOR
We have saved Ilium this long time. We are enough.

CHORUS LEADER
Are you so sure you have the enemy beaten now?   330

HECTOR
I am so sure. God's daylight, which is near, will show.

CHORUS LEADER

Look to the future. God often reverses fortunes.

HECTOR

I hate a man who comes too late to help his friends.
As for this man, since he is here, let him be here°
as a stranger guest at our table, but as no fighting man.   335
He has lost all the kind feelings of the sons of Troy.

CHORUS LEADER

Spurn allies, lord, and you gain peril and lose love.

SHEPHERD

If the enemy only saw him they would be afraid.

HECTOR   (To Chorus Leader.)

You urge me faithfully.

                                              (To Shepherd.)

And you have given a timely report.
So, for the sake of what the messenger has said,   340
let golden-armored Rhesus join us as our ally.

                                        (Exit Shepherd to the side.)

CHORUS [singing]

STROPHE A

Adrasteia: Necessity: Zeus'
daughter! Keep bad luck from my mouth.
For I will speak what is in my heart.
All I wish shall be spoken.   345
You are here, child of the River,
here, at long last now in the court of Friendship,
and welcome, since it was long, before
the Muse your mother and the grand-bridged
river god sent you to help us.   350

ANTISTROPHE A

This was Strymon, who with the Muse

melodious, in the clear shining
and watery swirl of their embrace,
begot your youth and glory.
You come, a Zeus resplendent   355
for show, driving behind your dappled horses.
Now, O my country, my Phrygia,
now, with god's will, you can claim the aid
of Zeus himself, Liberator.

Will it ever happen again that our ancient Troy   360
will know the day-long revelries,
the love pledge and companionship,
the strumming on the lyres and the wine cups circling,
passed to the right, in sweet contention,
while on the open water the sons
of Atreus make for Sparta,   365
gone from the shores of Ilium?
O friend, could it only be
that with hand and spear you would do
this before you leave us!

O come, appear, lift and flourish your golden buckler,   370
slant it across the eyes of Peleus' son, over
the split chariot-rail, spur on your colts, then
cast the two-pointed spear. None
who stands against you shall dance   375
ever again on the level lands
of Argive Hera. He shall die
here, by a Thracian death, a welcome
weight on this land, which will take him.

(Enter Rhesus from the side.)

[chanting]
Great King, he comes, O great King.
Gallant, O Thrace,   380

is this youngling you bred, a monarch to behold.
See the great force on his gold-armored body,
hear the brave noise of his clashing bells
that jangle on the shield rim.
A god, O Troy, a god, a real Ares   385
is this stallion sired by the singing Muse
and Strymon, who comes to inspire you.

RHESUS

Great son of a great father, monarch of this land,
O Hector, hail. On this late day I greet you,
and greet the good success that finds you so advanced   390
against the enemy's camp. Now I am here to help
you knock their walls to rubble and to burn their ships.

HECTOR

O son of a melodious mother, one of the Nine,
and Strymon, the River of Thrace: it is my way
always to speak the truth. I have no diplomacy.   395
Long, long ago you should have come to help our struggle.
For all you have done, Troy could have fallen to Greek arms.
This should not be.
You cannot say it was because your friends never called you
that you did not come, and did not help, and paid no heed.   400
What herald or what aged representatives
did not arrive to entreat you to our city's help?
What honorable gifts did we not send? For all
you did, you might as well have thrown us to the Greeks,
though you and we are non-Greek, one barbarian blood.   405
Yet it was I who with this hand made you so great
and lord of Thrace, though you were but a small chieftain
before I swept Pangaeum and Paeonia,
fought with the Thracian warriors face to face, and broke
their lines of bucklers, made slaves of their people, turned 410
them over to you. You owe us much. You have spurned it
and to your friends in distress come with late relief.
Yet here are others, who are not our kin by blood,

who came long ago, and some of them have fallen and lie
buried in their mounds, who greatly kept faith with our city,   415
while others, in their armor, by their chariot teams,
have stood whatever cold winds or thirsty heat the god
sends, and still do endure it, without
sleeping, as you did, snug beneath the covers,
or drinking deep your wine and toasting one another.
There, you may know that Hector speaks his mind.   420
I have my grievance, and I tell you to your face.

RHESUS

I am another such as you. I cut a path
straight through arguments. I too have no diplomacy.
But I have been hurt more at the heart than you, more vexed
and shamed, not to be here in your country.   425
But see. There is a land neighbor to mine, its people
are Scythian, and as I was about to keep appointment
at Ilium, these attacked me. I had reached the shores
of the Hostile Sea, to put my Thracian army across,
and there the ground was sopped with Scythian blood, and
    Thracian   430
too, as the spearwork made commingled slaughter.
Such were the accidents that kept me from my march
to Troy's plain and my arrival as your ally.
Once I had beaten them, made hostages of their children,
and set a yearly tribute to be paid to us,   435
I crossed the sea gate with my ships, went on by land
over the intervening country, and so am here;
not, as you claim, because I drank in comfort, not
because I slept at leisure in a golden house.
For I know well, I have endured them, those stiff winds   440
of ice that sweep Paeonia and the Thracian Sea.
Sleepless, and in this cloak here, I have come through these.
I come to you behind my time, but timely still,
for here is the tenth summer of your years of war,

and *you* have made no progress, but day after day   445
you throw your dice against the hazard of Argive arms;
one single day of sunlight is enough for *me*
to storm their walls and burst upon their mooringsteads
and kill the Achaeans. On the next day after that
I am off for home, having disposed of your whole war.   450
Not one of your people needs to lift a single shield.
I will deal with these vaunted Achaeans with my spear,
and destroy them, even though I came behind my time.

CHORUS [*singing*]

STROPHE A

Hail, hail,
welcome your cry, welcome, you come from Zeus, only I pray   455
that Zeus keep away
the invincible spirit of Envy from cursing your words.
For no man from Argos
did the sea armament bring, before   460
or now, stronger than you. Say how
could even Achilles endure your spear?
How could Ajax endure it?
If I could only see, my lord, only see that day
when your spear hand   465
is bloody with retribution.

RHESUS

So for my too-long absence I will make amends
thus (but may Adrasteia not resent my words):
when we have liberated this city of yours and when
you have chosen first spoils and devoted them to the gods,   470
I am willing to sail with you against the Argives, storm
and ravage the whole land of Hellas with our spears,
to let them learn what it is like to be attacked.

HECTOR

If I could only get rid of my present troubles

and rule a peaceful city as I did before 475
I would be very grateful to the gods.
As for the Argive country and the Greek domain,
they are not so easy to devastate as you seem to think.

RHESUS

Do they not say the greatest of the Greeks are here?

HECTOR

They are great enough for me. I want no more. 480

RHESUS

Then, once we have killed these, have we not done
everything?

HECTOR

Don't plan for distant ventures before finishing what's at
hand.

RHESUS

You seem content to be acted on, not to act.

HECTOR

I have my own kingdom here, and it is large.
Now, whether you want the left wing, or the right, 485
or to be among the central allies, take your choice,
and plant your shields, station your army where you wish.

RHESUS

My wish, Hector, is to fight the enemy alone;
but if you think it shame to take no hand in burning
their beached ships, an end for which you fought so long, 490
set me face to face with Achilles and his men.

HECTOR

It is not possible to set your eager spears
against him.

RHESUS

                    The story was he sailed to Troy.

HECTOR

He sailed. He is here. But angry
with their generals, he takes no part in the fighting.   495

RHESUS

Who is most famous in their army after him?

HECTOR

Ajax, I think, is just as good, and Tydeus' son
Diomedes. Then there is that talker, that big mouth,
Odysseus, but his heart is brave enough, who has done
more damage to our country than any single man.   500
He it was who crept in the night to Athena's shrine
and stole her image and took it to the Argive ships.
There was a time the Argives sent him to scout us,
and in a beggar's miserable outfit, disguised,
he got inside our walls, railing against the Greeks.   505
But then he killed the sentries and the gate guards and got
    free
away. Constantly he is observed, under cover
by the Thymbraean altar, near the city, watching
his chance. A crafty planner, always a handful of trouble.

RHESUS

Why, no true man of spirit deigns to kill his man   510
by stealth. One should go forward and attack direct.
This man you speak of, crouching in thievish ambuscades
and scheming stratagems, this man I will seize alive,
impale him through the spine where the road goes out the
    gates,
and leave him there to feed the vultures.   515
That is the kind of death that such a man should die
for being a low brigand and a temple robber.

HECTOR

Well, it is night now, and time for you to bivouac.
I will show you your place, apart from where the rest
of the army is stationed. There your men can spend the night.   520

Should you want anything, the watchword is "Phoebus."
Learn it. Remember. Tell it to your Thracian force.

(To the Chorus.)

Now, you must go out in advance of our position,
keep a sharp watch, and be on the lookout for Dolon
who's scouting the ships, for, if he is still alive,   525
he must be almost back now to the Trojan camp.

(Exit Hector and Rhesus to the side.)

CHORUS [*singing*]

STROPHE B

Whose is the watch now? Who relieves
mine? The early constellations
are setting. The Pleiades' sevenfold course
rides high, and the Eagle soars in the center of heaven.   530
Wake. What keeps you? Wake
from your sleep, to your watch.
Do you not see how the moon shines?
Dawn is near, dawn   535
is breaking now, here is the star
that runs before it.
[*The next few lines are chanted by various Chorus members*]

CHORUS LEADER
Who was announced for the first watch?

CHORUS MEMBER
Coroebus, they say, Mygdon's son.

CHORUS LEADER
Who was after that?

CHORUS MEMBER
                    The Paeonian force   540
awoke the Cilicians. Mysians awoke us.

CHORUS LEADER
Then is it not time to go wake the Lycians

and take the fifth
watch in our turn as allotted? 545

CHORUS [*singing*]

ANTISTROPHE B

I hear. But perched above Simois
the nightingale,
the own-child-slayer in vociferous chant
sings her murderous marriage, sings her song and her sorrow. 550
The flocks are pasturing on Ida
now. I can hear the night-murmuring
call of the shepherd's pipe.
Sleep is a magic on my eyes.
It comes sweetest 555
to the lids about dawn.

[*Again, the following lines are chanted by different Chorus members*]

CHORUS LEADER

Why is the scout not here, that one
Hector sent to spy on their ships?

CHORUS MEMBER

I fear for him. He is long gone.

CHORUS LEADER

Might he have stumbled into an ambush 560
and been killed?

CHORUS MEMBER

He might. It is to be feared.°

CHORUS LEADER

My orders are to go wake the Lycians
and take the fifth
watch in our turn as allotted.

(*Exit the Chorus to the side. Then enter Odysseus and Diomedes
cautiously from the side, bearing Dolon's armor.*)

ODYSSEUS

Diomedes, did you hear? Or was it a noise without 565
meaning that falls on my ears? Some clash of armor?

DIOMEDES

It was nothing, the jangle of iron on the harness
against the chariot rails. But I was frightened too,
at first, when I heard the clanking of the metal.

ODYSSEUS

Be careful. You might run into their sentries in the dark. 570

DIOMEDES

I will watch how I step despite the darkness.

ODYSSEUS

If you do wake anyone, do you know what their watchword is?

DIOMEDES

I know it. It's "Phoebus." Dolon told me.

ODYSSEUS

Look!
Here are some bivouacs of the enemy. But empty.

DIOMEDES

Dolon spoke of this too. He said Hector should be sleeping 575
here. And it is for Hector that this sword is drawn.

ODYSSEUS

What can it mean? Perhaps the troops have gone somewhere?

DIOMEDES

He may have gone to work some stratagem against us.

ODYSSEUS

Hector is bold, very bold, now that he is winning.

DIOMEDES

What shall we do now, Odysseus? We hoped to find 580
our man asleep, but we've failed.

ODYSSEUS

We must go back to our mooring place as quick as we can.
Whatever god it is who grants him his success
is watching over him now. We must not force Fortune.

DIOMEDES

But should we not look for Aeneas? Or for that Phrygian   585
we hate worst of all, Paris? Cut their heads off?

ODYSSEUS

How, without deadly peril, can you find these men
in the dark, and here among our enemies?

DIOMEDES

But it is shameful to go back to the Argive ships
without doing our enemies the least damage.   590

ODYSSEUS

How can you say you have done no damage? Did we not kill
Dolon, who scouted our ships? Do we not carry his armor
here, our spoils? Do you think you can sack their whole
    camp?

DIOMEDES

You are right. Let us go back. May we only succeed!

(Enter Athena above the tent.)

ATHENA

Where are you going? Why do you leave the Trojan camp   595
biting your very hearts for disappointed spite
because the god will not allow you to kill their Hector
or their Paris? Have you not heard of the ally,
Rhesus, who has come to Troy in no mean circumstance?
For if he survives this night and is alive tomorrow,   600
not even Achilles, and not Ajax with his spear,
can keep him from destroying all the Argive fleet,
smashing, demolishing your walls and storming in
to fight with level spears.

Kill him, and all is won. Let Hector bivouac   605
in peace, nor try to murder him.
His death shall come, but it shall come from another hand.

ODYSSEUS

Athena, mistress, for I recognized your voice
and way of speaking that I know so well, and know
how you are always with me and watch over me,   610
tell me, where is this man sleeping whom you bid us
attack? Where is his station in the Trojan camp?

ATHENA

He is camped right here and has not joined the main army.
Hector gave him this place to sleep, outside the lines,
until this night passes and day comes, and by him   615
are picketed the horses from the Thracian
chariots, so white that you can see them through the dark
gleaming, as if they were the wings of swans on water.
Kill their master and bring these home to your camp,
spoils of surpassing splendor, for no place on earth   620
contains a team of chariot horses such as these.

ODYSSEUS

Diomedes, yours be the work of killing Thracians—
or let me do it, and you look after the horses.

DIOMEDES

I will do the killing; you manage the horses.
You are the experienced one, the quick improviser.   625
One ought to place a man where he can do most good.

ATHENA

Alexander is here, I see him, coming our way
in haste. He must have heard from one of the guards
confused rumors about the presence of enemies.

DIOMEDES

Does he have others with him or is he by himself?   630

ATHENA

He's alone. He seems to be making for where Hector sleeps,
so he can report to him the presence of spies in the camp.

DIOMEDES

Well, should he not be killed and his account settled?

ATHENA

No. You must not go beyond what has been destined for you.
There is no authority for you to kill this man.   635
You came here, bringing their destined death to certain
  others.
Do it. Dispatch. Now to this man I shall pretend
I'm Aphrodite, his ally, standing beside him
in all perils. I'll pay him back with rotten lies.
This I have said. But though my victim stands close by   640
he's heard and knows nothing of what's in store for him.

> (*Exit Diomedes and Odysseus to one side,*
> *enter Alexander from the other.*)

ALEXANDER

Hector, my general, my brother, Hector I say,
are you sleeping? How can you sleep? Waken, will you?
Here is some enemy got close inside our lines;
someone has come to rob us, or to spy on us.   645

ATHENA

Fear not. Here is your faithful ally Aphrodite
watching over you. Your war is my war. I do not forget
your favor and your kindness to me. I am grateful,
and now, to your Trojan army in its high success
I come, bringing a friend and mighty man of war,   650
the Thracian, child of that divine maker of melodies,
the Muse herself; the River Strymon is named his father.°

ALEXANDER

Always you are in truth the good friend of my city

and me. I think the best thing I ever did
in my life was to judge you first and win you to my city.   655
What brings me here—there are wild rumors flying about
among the sentries, nothing clear. Achaean spies,
they say, are among us. One man reports but has not seen
    them;
another saw them coming but knows nothing else
about it. This is why I came to Hector's quarters.   660

ATHENA

Never fear. There's nothing wrong in the camp.
Hector is gone to give the Thracians a place to sleep.

ALEXANDER

I trust you. I always believe what you say. I'll go
and keep my station, free of this anxiety.

ATHENA

Go, for your interests are always on my mind,   665
and all my purpose is to see my friends succeed.
Oh, you will learn soon how I shall take care of you.

                                    (Exit Alexander to one side.)

        (Calling offstage to the other side to Odysseus and Diomedes.)

You two, over there. You are too bold. You, I am calling
you, son of Laertes, put your sharp sword away.
Our Thracian captain's down.   670
We have his horses, but the enemy are aware
and coming at you. Now is the time for speed, speed,
to run for where the ships are moored. What keeps you?
The enemy are upon you. Save your lives.

                    *(Exit Athena. Enter from one side Odysseus and Diomedes,
                         from the other the Chorus of Trojan guards.)*

CHORUS [*singing*]
There they go, there!°
Shoot, shoot.   675

Spear them.
Who is it? Look! That's the man I mean.
They have come to rob us in the night, and they have roused the
camp.
This way all.   680
Here they are. We have them fast.
What's your regiment? Where do you come from? Who are you?

ODYSSEUS

Nothing for you to know. You have done an evil day's work.
You shall die.

CHORUS LEADER

Tell me the watchword, will you, before you get this spear
stuck
through your chest.

ODYSSEUS

Stop. There's no danger.

CHORUS LEADER

Bring him here. Now, everyone, strike him.   685

ODYSSEUS

Was it you killed Rhesus?

CHORUS LEADER

No. You tried to kill him. We'll kill *you!*

ODYSSEUS

Hold hard everyone.

CHORUS LEADER

We will not.

ODYSSEUS

Hold. You must not kill a friend.

CHORUS LEADER

What's the watchword?

ODYSSEUS

Phoebus.

CHORUS LEADER

I acknowledge it. Down spears all.
Do you know where those men have got to?

ODYSSEUS

Yes, I saw them go this way.

(He points to one side.)

CHORUS LEADER

On their trail, then, everyone.
　　　　　Should we raise a general alarm?　　　　　690
No. It would be bad to disturb our friends with an alarm in
　　the night.

*(Exit Odysseus and Diomedes to one side; the Chorus
starts to go off to the other but hesitates.)*

CHORUS [*singing*]

STROPHE

Who was the man who was here?
Who is it so hardy that he shall boast
that he escaped my hand?
Where shall I find him now?　　　　　695
What shall I think he can be,
that man who came on fearless foot through the dark
across the stations of our ranks and our guards?
Some Thessalian
or some dweller in a seaside Locrian city?　　　　　700
One whose living is made on the scattered islands?
Who was it? Where did he come from? What country?
Which god does he acknowledge as god supreme?

CHORUS LEADER [*speaking*]

Was this the work of Odysseus after all? Or whose?
If we are to judge by past deeds, who else?　　　　　705

CHORUS MEMBER [singing]
    You think so?

CHORUS LEADER [singing]
      I must do.

CHORUS MEMBER
    He has been bold against us!

CHORUS MEMBER
    Bold? Who? Whom are you praising?

CHORUS MEMBER
        Odysseus.

CHORUS LEADER [speaking]
    Never praise him, that thief, that treacherous fighter.

CHORUS [singing]

ANTISTROPHE

He came once before   710
into our citadel, bleary-eyed
and huddled in a disguise
of rags, his sword hand
hidden under his clothes,
begging his bread he crept in, a wretched vagrant,   715
dirty, unkempt, foul,
and much evil he spoke
against the royal house of the sons of Atreus
as if he hated all the lords of their host.
I wish he had died, died as he deserved   720
before he ever set foot on the Phrygian shore.

CHORUS LEADER
    Whether it was Odysseus or not, I am afraid.
    We are the sentries, and Hector will hold us to blame.

CHORUS MEMBER [singing]
    With what charge?

CHORUS LEADER [*singing*]
With curses ...

CHORUS MEMBER
For doing what? What do you fear?   725

CHORUS LEADER
               ... because they got through us.

CHORUS MEMBER
               Who did?

CHORUS LEADER [*now speaking*]
Those men who got into the Phrygian camp tonight.

CHARIOTEER OF RHESUS [*from the side, singing*]
Oh god. Disaster!

CHORUS LEADER
Listen!
Silence. Keep your places all. Perhaps someone is in our nets.   730

(*Enter Charioteer of Rhesus, wounded, from the side.*)

CHARIOTEER OF RHESUS
Halloo, help!
Disaster and ruin for the Thracians.

CHORUS LEADER
               This is one of our allies
in pain or terror.

CHARIOTEER OF RHESUS [*chanting throughout the following
interchange*]
Halloo!
I am hurt, I am done. And you, lord of the Thracians,
how hateful that day you saw Troy,
what an end to your life.   735

CHORUS LEADER
You must be one of our allies, but who? My eyes
fail me in the dark. I cannot clearly make you out.

CHARIOTEER OF RHESUS

Where can I find some chief of the Trojans?
Where is Hector himself?
Drowsing somewhere, sleeping under arms?   740
Is there none in command to whom I can report
what happened to us, what someone has done
and got clean away, vanished, leaving plain to see
the hurt he inflicted on the Thracians?

CHORUS LEADER

Some mishap has come to the Thracian force, it seems   745
from what this man says.

CHARIOTEER OF RHESUS

The army is shattered, the king is killed
by a traitor's stroke,
and oh, my own wound hurts   750
deep and bleeds. Shall I die? Must both
Rhesus and I be basely killed
in Troy, which we came to help?

CHORUS LEADER

There is no mystery in the ill news he reports
now; it is plain to see that our allies are killed.   755

CHARIOTEER OF RHESUS [*now speaking*]

There has been wickedness done here. More than wickedness:
shame too, which makes the evil double its own bulk.
To die with glory, if one has to die at all,
is still, I think, pain for the dier, surely so,
yet grandeur left for his survivors, honor for his house.   760
But death to us came senseless and inglorious.
When Hector with his own hand led us to our quarters
and gave us the watchword, we lay down to sleep, worn out
with the fatigue of our long march. No one kept watch
in our contingent for that night, nor were our arms   765
stacked out in order, nor were the goads in place beside
the yokes of the horses, since our king had been assured

that you were masters of the field and your pickets threatened
their anchorage; so we dropped in our tracks, and grossly
   slept.
Yet my own heart was restless, and I woke again   770
to give some fodder to the horses, thinking we must
harness them for the dawn's fighting, so I heaped their food
lavishly. Now I see two fellows stealing through our camp
in the dense dark, but when I started in their direction
they dodged away and made off.   775
I called out and warned them to stay away from the camp.
I thought some of our allies had gone out to steal
from us.
      No reply.
          I did not give it another thought.
I went back to where I had been, and slept again.
But now there came an apparition to my sleep.   780
Those horses, that I trained and drove as charioteer
at Rhesus' side, I saw them, as one sees in a dream,
but wolves had got astride their backs and rode them now,
and stabbed their backs and rumps with their tails as goads—
   the mares
went wild with terror, bucking and fighting, snorting   785
from flared nostrils.
I started up to drive those savage beasts away
from the mares, for the dream's terror had awakened me.
As I raised my head I heard a moan such as men make
when they die, and a jet of hot fresh blood splashed me. It
   came   790
from my master, who had been murdered, and died hard.
I leapt upright, but there was no spear in my hand,
and as I looked about and fumbled for a weapon
somebody coming close up slashed me hard in the side
with a sword. I took and felt a cut from the blade   795
that ripped me deep.
I fell on my face. He and the other man seized the team
and car, mounted, galloped away, and escaped.

Ah.

I am faint from my wound, I cannot stand.
I know what happened, for I saw it, but do not   800
understand in what way these men could have been killed
nor what hand killed them. I can guess.
My guess is that our friends were the ones who hurt us.

CHORUS LEADER

O charioteer of that unfortunate Thracian king,
do not be angry with us. The enemy did this.   805

(Enter Hector from the side.)

And here is Hector in person, who has heard the news
and comes, I think, in sympathy for your misfortune.

HECTOR   (To the Chorus.)

You are responsible for a disaster. How did it happen
that these marauders sent out by the enemy
got past you and made havoc in our camp? Disgraceful!   810
Why did you not shout out loud as they came in
nor as they were going out? Someone will pay for this,
and who but you? I hold you responsible. You had the watch.
Now they are gone, untouched, and much amused, no doubt,
with the feebleness of the Trojans, and of me, their leader.   815
I tell you now—father Zeus be witness to my oath—
death by flogging or by the headsman's axe awaits you
for your part in this. Else, say Hector is a weakling.
Say he is nothing.

CHORUS [singing]

ANTISTROPHE A

No, no!   820
We came to you, lord, defender of the city, we did,°
we came (it must have been these),
we told you their fires were burning beside the ships.
Since then, all through the night's vigil   825
our eyes have not deadened, they have not slept;
by the springs of Simois we swear it. O my lord,

do not be angry with us. None of all this
that has happened is our fault.
If again, in the course of time, you prove we have said or done   830
anything wrong, then bury us
alive in the ground. We will not protest.

CHARIOTEER OF RHESUS   *(To Hector.)*

You are a barbarian, so are we. Why do you parry
my charge by threatening these men? Why make a Greek
lawyer's speech here?
You did this.
        We Thracians,   835
the wounded and the dead, will not be satisfied
with anyone else. It would take you a long and artful speech
to convince me that you have not been killing your friends.
You coveted those horses. For their sake, you murdered
your own allies, whose coming you had begged so hard.   840
They did come. They are dead. When Paris shamed hospitality
he was better than you—you murderer of your friends and
    helpers.
Never tell me it was one of the Argives
got through to destroy us. Who could slip through the Trojan
    lines
without detection and reach us?   845
You and the whole of the Phrygian army lay between.
Who of your own particular allies is dead,
or wounded, by those enemies you speak of? We
who lay beyond are wounded, some, while others fared worse
and do not look any longer on the light of the sun.   850
I tell you plain. I do not think this was any Achaean.
Who could pick a path through the enemy in the dark
and find where Rhesus lay—unless they were directed
by a god? They would not even know
of his arrival. Your defense is artificial.   855

HECTOR

We have had the help of our allies through all the time

that the Achaean army has been on our shores,
and not one word of complaint has come from any of them
of ill treatment. You would be the first. I hope
no greed for horses ever makes me kill my friends   860
to get them. This is more of Odysseus. What man else
among the Argives could have planned and done it?
I fear him. The thought, too, racks my mind,
he might have chanced to meet Dolon and killed him. Dolon
has been gone for a long time, and there's no sign of him.   865

CHARIOTEER OF RHESUS
I don't know what "Odysseuses" you're talking about.
I do know we're hurt, and it was no enemy did it.

HECTOR
Since you cannot think otherwise, then go on thinking this.

CHARIOTEER OF RHESUS
O land of my fathers, how can I reach you, and there die?

HECTOR
No dying. Too many have died already.   870

CHARIOTEER OF RHESUS
I have lost my masters. Where shall I turn to?

HECTOR
My own house will take you in and make you well.

CHARIOTEER OF RHESUS
How shall the hands of our murderers take care of me?

HECTOR
This man keeps saying the same thing. He will not stop.

CHARIOTEER OF RHESUS
Perish the murderer. I do not mean you;   875
you need not protest. The spirit of Justice knows who did it.

HECTOR
Take him up. Help him into my house,

then look after him carefully, so that he will not
be complaining any more.

(Exit Charioteer of Rhesus, assisted, to the side.)

(To the Chorus.)

You go to the forces on the wall,
to Priam and the elders. Tell them it is time   880
to bury these dead beside the highway where it leaves
our city.

CHORUS [*chanting*]
After our high success, does the god
now change Troy's luck, bring us back, to suffer
new losses? What does he plan?

(The Chorus starts to go off to one side but stops when the Muse
appears above, holding in her arms the body of Rhesus.)

But see, see,   885
my king, over your head, what goddess
hovers, carrying aloft in her arms
the man lately slain?
A pitiful sight. It fills me with fear.

THE MUSE
Behold me, Trojans, and fear not. I am the Muse,   890
one of the Nine and prized among the poets, who stand
before you. I have seen the death of my dear son
so sadly slain by the enemy. His killer, treacherous
Odysseus, some day shall be punished as he deserves.

[*now singing*]

STROPHE
With our own song of mourning   895
I mourn you, my child. Oh, you hurt
your mother when you went
that day to Troy,
a cursed, wretched way.

I would not have had you go, but you went.   900
Your father restrained you, but you broke away.
I mourn you, my child, dear,
dearest heart, I mourn you.

CHORUS LEADER

I, too, as much as ever one can grieve
who has no kinship with the dead, grieve for your son.   905

THE MUSE [still singing]

ANTISTROPHE

Perish the grandson of Oeneus.
Perish the son of Laertes.
He made me childless, who had
the best child in the world.
Perish the woman who forsook   910
her Greek home for a Phrygian bed.
She, dearest son, she is your true destroyer,
she, who made unnumbered cities
empty of the brave.

[now speaking]

Philammon's son, both when you lived and when you died   915
you have struck my heart and wounded me deeply, O
    Thamyris.
Rude violence did all. It brought you down. Your challenge
to the Muses, too, made me bear this unhappy son;
for as I waded through the waters of the Strymon,
the river god was on me; I was in his arms   920
and conceived. It was when we Muses, all arrayed
with our instruments, went to the gold-soiled mountain-
    mass
of Pangaeum, and the high contest of melody
with that great Thracian singer, and we blinded him,
Thamyris, who had vilified our craft of song.   925
When you were born, in shame over my maidenhood
and before my sisters, I flung you into the great waters
of your father, and Strymon gave you into the care

of no mortals, but the maiden nymphs of his own springs
who nursed you to perfection and then sent you forth,   930
child, to be king of Thrace and first of mortal men.
There in the bloody valors of your land's defense
I never feared your death.
Only to Troy I warned you, you must never go
knowing what waited you there, but Hector's embassies   935
and the repeated conclaves of the men of state
persuaded you to come to the defense of friends.
Athena! You alone are guilty of this death.
Odysseus and the son of Tydeus were your agents;
without you they did nothing. Never think I do not know.   940
And yet I and my sister Muses make your Athens
great in our art, and by our presence in the land;
and it was Orpheus, own first cousin to this man
you have slain, who first instructed your people in the rites
of mystery and secrets revealed; last, it was we   945
the sisters who with Phoebus educated
Musaeus, your great and respected citizen,
so he surpassed all other singers.
Here is your gratitude. I hold my son in my arms
and mourn him.
    I need no other expert to sing with me.

CHORUS LEADER

Hector, that Thracian charioteer with his mad charge   950
that we plotted Rhesus' murder is proved wrong.

HECTOR

I knew that well. It took no divination
to see the hand of Odysseus in this warrior's death.
And as for my part, when I saw the Greek army camped
on our shores, what should I do but send my heralds out   955
to our allies and ask them to come and help?
I sent heralds. This man was in my debt. He came to help.
But do not think I am unmoved by his death.
I am also ready to make him a great funeral mound

and burn the glory of innumerable robes.   960
He was my friend. He came to help. And now he's dead.

THE MUSE

Rhesus will not go to the black meadow in the earth.
So much at least I claim from the infernal bride,
the daughter of Demeter, goddess of the fields,
that she send up his soul. She is in debt to me   965
to show that she gives honor to the friends of Orpheus.
For me he will be as one dead, with no more light
in his eyes, for the rest of time. He will not come again
to where he looks upon his mother any more.
Hidden deep in the caves among the silver mines   970
under the ground he shall live on, a human spirit,
seeing the light as prophet of Bacchus, who made his shrine
under Pangaeum's cliff, a holy god for initiates.
The load of grief that I must bear is lighter
than that of the sea goddess. Her son too must die.   975
I with my sisters first shall lament your death, my son,
then mourn Achilles, on Thetis' day of sorrow.
Pallas, who killed you, cannot save him.
Apollo's quiver holds the shaft that means his death.
O making of children, hapless work, sorrow of mankind,   980
the man who reasons well
will live his whole life childless and not risk having
    children
whom some day he must bury.

                                        (*Exit the Muse.*)

CHORUS LEADER

Rhesus is in his mother's hands, and she will mourn him.
Hector, your work lies now before you. It is dawn.   985
It is time. What would you have us do?

HECTOR

About your business. Tell the allies to arm with speed,
and yoke their horses to the chariots,

then, when full armed, await the call of the Tyrrhenian
trumpet. For I am confident we can overrun
the camp and walls of the Achaeans, fire their ships,   990
and that this sunlight that begins to climb
brings us of Troy our day of liberty.

(Exit to the side.)

CHORUS LEADER [*chanting*]
　Obey the king. Let us march, well armed,
　in good order, give the word
　to the allies. Who knows? The god who is on our side   995
　might grant us the victory.

TEXTUAL NOTES

(Line numbers are in some cases only approximate.)

THE BACCHAE

72–82: Euripides' language here employs some traditional elements of ceremonial Greek "blessing" (*makarismos*), and William Arrowsmith's original translation of these lines used Christian language, especially from the Beatitudes in the (King James) Authorized Version of the New Testament, to convey something of the sacral fervor of the chorus:

> —Blessèd, blessèd are those who know the mysteries of god.
> —Blessèd is he who hallows his life in the worship of god,
>   he whom the spirit of god possesseth, who is one
>   with those who belong to the holy body of god.   75
> —Blessèd are the dancers and those who are purified,
>   who dance on the hill in the holy dance of god.
> —Blessèd are they who keep the rite of Cybele the Mother.
> —Blessèd are the thyrsus-bearers, those who wield in their hands
>   the holy wand of god.   80
> —Blessèd are those who wear the crown of the ivy of god.
> —Blessèd, blessèd are they: Dionysus is their god!

151: The text of this line is uncertain.

182: This line is similar to line 860 and is rejected by some scholars as an interpolation here.

200: Some scholars assign this line to Cadmus. Possibly one line may have dropped out after it.

315: Text uncertain.

316: This line is identical to *Hippolytus* 80 and is rejected by many scholars here as an interpolation.

428–29: The text of these lines is uncertain, though their sense is clear.

506: The text of these words is suspect.

540: Before this line the manuscripts transmit the words "What fury, what fury!"; they are rejected by most modern scholars as an ungrammatical interpolation.

585: This word is missing in the manuscripts and is supplied by modern scholars.

606: The text of the last part of this line is uncertain.

631: This word is missing in the manuscripts and is supplied by modern scholars.

652: A line has almost certainly been lost in the manuscript, most likely containing Dionysus' reply to Pentheus' disparagement of the god in line 652; on this assumption, the words "The god himself will come to teach you wisdom" give one possible indication of what might have been lost. But some scholars instead assign line 652 to Dionysus and suggest that the line that has been lost was the previous one, containing Pentheus' retort in response to Dionysus' praise of the god in line 651.

673: This line is similar to one transmitted as part of a quotation from a lost play of Euripides and is rejected here by some scholars as an interpolation.

716: This line is similar to line 667 and is rejected here by many scholars as an interpolation.

757: This sentence seems out of place here and is transposed by many scholars, with some changes, to follow after line 761.

842: Two half lines seem to have been lost here.

877: Text and meaning of this line are uncertain.

896: Text and meaning of this line are uncertain.

973–76: Either Pentheus exits before these lines and does not hear them; or else he is still on stage but is so dazed that he does not seem to hear or understand them. Given that Dionysus leads him throughout this whole episode, the latter alternative seems likelier.

996–1010: Arrowsmith's original translation of this antistrophe elaborates freely upon the themes suggested by the very uncertain and difficult Greek text:

—Uncontrollable, the unbeliever goes,
    in spitting rage, rebellious and amok,

madly assaulting the mysteries of god,
profaning the rites of the mother of god.
Against the unassailable he runs, with rage   1000
obsessed. Headlong he runs to death.
For death the gods exact, curbing by that bit
the mouths of men. They humble us with death
that we remember what we are who are not god,
but men. We run to death. Wherefore, I say,
accept, accept:
humility is wise; humility is blest.
But what the world calls wise I do not want.   1005
Elsewhere the chase. I hunt another game,
those great, those manifest, those certain goals,
achieving which, our mortal lives are blest.
Let these things be the quarry of my chase:
purity; humility; an unrebellious soul,
accepting all. Let me go the customary way,
the timeless, honored, beaten path of those who walk
with reverence and awe beneath the sons of heaven.   1010

1002–7: The meter and meaning of these lines are very uncertain.

1025–26: These lines are rejected by some scholars as an interpolation.

1028: This line is similar to *Medea* 54 and is rejected by many scholars here as an interpolation.

1036: The rest of this line and probably one more following line are missing in the manuscript.

1060: The translation reflects the text of the manuscript; many editors accept a modern scholarly emendation that yields the sense, "I cannot see their frantic illnesses."

1090: After this line the medieval manuscript has two lines that are missing in an ancient papyrus and that are rejected by modern scholars: "running with intense runnings of the feet, mother Agave and her kindred sisters."

1158: The text of these last words is uncertain.

1174: Most of a line is missing here.

1221: After this line the manuscript transmits a line that has been omitted here: "having picked them up where they were lying in a forest difficult to search."

1244-45: One or both of these lines are rejected by many scholars as an interpolation.

1301: At least one line containing Cadmus' reply to Agave, and probably rather more, has been lost here.

1329: Scholars use the following sources to reconstruct the missing section of the play: (1) one of the hypotheses (ancient scholarly summaries) of the play, according to which "Dionysus appeared and then addressed all of them and revealed to each one what would happen to him or her" (there follow some corrupt words); (2) Apsines, a third-century CE rhetorician, who writes, "In Euripides, Pentheus' mother Agave is freed from her madness and recognizes her son who has been torn apart; then she accuses herself and arouses pity.... Euripides deploys this rhetorical device because he wishes to arouse commiseration for Pentheus: the mother takes up each of his limbs in her hands and laments each one in turn"; (3) *Christus Patiens* (*The Passion of Christ*), an anonymous Byzantine cento (a poetic text consisting entirely of citations from famous works by earlier poets) which is probably to be dated to the twelfth century, and containing a number of lines that have been attributed with more or less probability to this play (especially lines 1011, 1120-23, 1256-57, 1312-13, 1449, and 1466-72 for Agave's speech; and 300, 1360-62, 1639-40, 1663-1679, 1690, and 1756 for Dionysus'); (4) a line quoted from the scholia (ancient commentary) on line 907 of Aristophanes' *Wealth* as coming from this play; and (5) a few very scrappy papyrus fragments.

1344, 1346, 1348: Some scholars assign these lines to Agave.

1351: It is not certain, but most likely, that Dionysus exits at this point. But see note on lines 1377-78.

1353: This word is missing in the manuscript and has been restored by modern scholars.

1372: After this line a line is missing containing the rest of Cadmus' reply to Agave; the words "burial place ... son on Cithaeron" give one possible indication of what has been lost.

1374-76: Text uncertain.

1377-78: The manuscript assigns these lines to Dionysus (who in that case did not exit after line 1351) and reads, "I was terribly blasphemed by you, / my name dishonored in Thebes"; the translation reflects a widely accepted modern scholarly emendation.

1385: Text uncertain.

1388-92: These lines are rejected by many scholars as non-Euripidean.

7–8: The manuscript assigns these lines to the Old Man, but all modern editors give them to Agamemnon.

115–20: The order of these verses in the manuscript is different; modern scholars have transposed them to yield a better sense.

149–51: The text and exact sense of these lines are uncertain.

261: The manuscript notes that two lines are missing here.

273: Modern scholars have noted that two lines are missing here.

284: The text of the last four words and their sense are uncertain.

290–91: Text uncertain.

317: At some point the Old Man must exit, but it is uncertain exactly when he does so. Some editors suggest that he may stay on the stage as late as line 542.

394A: This line is missing in the manuscript and is supplied by modern scholars from ancient citations; it is numbered 394a because it had not yet been added when the standard line numbering was established in the Renaissance.

521: The text of this line is uncertain; the sense given by the translation is conjectural.

564–65: Text uncertain and meaning unclear.

570–71: The text of the ending of this antistrophe is uncertain.

572: The text of the beginning of this epode is uncertain.

589: The text of the end of the epode is uncertain.

590–97: A few editors assign these lines to a second chorus of Argives who enter accompanying Clytemnestra and Iphigenia.

633–34: Many editors transpose these lines to follow 630 so that they conclude Clytemnestra's speech and so that Iphigenia speaks continuously from lines 631 to line 637.

652: Some editors delete this line and line 665 and transpose lines 662–65 to put them here.

662–65: See note on line 652.

666: Text uncertain.

667: The text of these last few words is uncertain.

682: This is the reading of the manuscript; many modern scholars print the modern scholarly emendation "you."

777: The text of these last several words is uncertain.

792: The text of these last several words is uncertain.

865: The text of this sentence and its meaning are very uncertain.

1022–23: Text uncertain.

1034: A word is missing here, presumably an adjective modifying "gods" ("intelligent"?).

1082–85: This passage is obscure and its text is uncertain. One plausible emendation would result in its meaning, "like a dappled deer from the rocky mountain caves or an unblemished heifer."

1151: Text uncertain.

1179: The text of the line containing this sentence and its meaning are uncertain.

1262–63: These two lines are inverted in the manuscript; what appears to be their correct sequence has been restored by modern scholars.

1301: Text uncertain.

1348: The text of Clytemnestra's question is uncertain.

1416: Most of this line is missing in the manuscript, and it cannot be known what it originally said; the translation is speculative.

1516–18: Text very uncertain.

1527: From here to the end of this choral song the text and its meaning are quite uncertain.

APPENDIX: For the problems involving the end of *Iphigenia in Aulis* as transmitted, see the introduction to the play. Aelian, an author of the fourth century CE, quotes from Euripides' *Iphigenia* the following lines, evidently addressed by Artemis *ex machina* either to Agamemnon or to Clytemnestra: "And I shall place in the dear hands of the Achaeans a doe / with horns; sacrificing this, they will suppose / that they are sacrificing your daughter."

66–67: This is the order of these two lines in the manuscript; most modern scholars invert them.

73–75: The text of these lines is uncertain.

146: Many scholars suspect that after this line two others have been lost, one for Odysseus and one for Silenus.

296: The text of these last words is uncertain.

343: The manuscript reads "fire and my father's bronze cauldron"; the translation reflects one possible correction.

374: A line is missing after this verse at the end of the antistrophe.

394: The text of this whole sentence is uncertain and its meaning is quite obscure.

399: A line may be missing after this line.

439–40: The text of these lines is uncertain and their meaning is controversial; the translation reflects one possibility.

480–82: Many scholars reject these lines as an interpolation.

513–15: The text of these lines is uncertain and one or two words are missing.

583: The manuscript reads "I'll sleep fine. By the Graces, I prefer boys to girls." The translation reflects a widely accepted scholarly emendation.

674: This manuscript reading is considered unacceptable by most scholars, but no satisfactory correction of it has as yet been found.

RHESUS

SCENE: A hypothesis (ancient scholarly summary) to *Rhesus* claims that two prologues to the play were extant, but neither one is found in our medieval manuscripts. One, apparently quoted by Dicaearchus (a Greek philosopher and student of Aristotle's, fourth to third century BCE), began, "Now the chariot-driven . . . the fair-moon gleam." The other, said to be found in some manuscripts, began, "O mighty child of greatest Zeus, / Pallas, what should we do? We should not / wait any longer to help the Achaeans' army. / For now they are doing badly in the spear battle, / suffering violently from Hector's spear. / There is no more painful grief for me, / ever since Alexander judged that the goddess Cypris / was greater in beauty than my own loveliness / and yours, Athena, dearest of the gods to me, / if I do not see the city of Priam razed to the ground, / utterly destroyed by force." On this whole question of the tragedy's prologue, see the introduction to the play.

1: The manuscripts as usual do not distinguish between the lines spoken or sung by the chorus as a group and those to be spoken by the chorus leader alone. In this play the leader seems to have a more definite actor's part then elsewhere in extant tragedy, especially at the beginning. Lines 1–10, for example, should probably be chanted by a single actor, not by a group; and this character must be the officer in charge of the detail, who is also the leader heading the chorus. We have therefore used our judgment in guessing where chanted lines are to be given to the chorus leader and where they should be given to the chorus.

16–18: Text uncertain.

37: After these words the manuscripts transmit two half lines (37–38): "Having left your sentry posts you are disturbing the army." These words are rejected by most scholars as an interpolation.

334–38. The order of these lines has been rearranged by modern scholars.

561–62: A few words are missing here.

652: This line is very similar to line 279 and is rejected by most scholars as an interpolation.

675–91: The distribution of singers and speakers in this scene is very uncertain; some modern scholars divide the sung lines among half choruses, others among individual members of the chorus. In addition, scholars disagree about the text to be adopted in a number of passages and whether the sequence of lines transmitted by the manuscripts is to be altered.

821–22: Text uncertain.

GLOSSARY

Achaea, Achaean(s): a region (and its people) in Greece on the northern coast of the Peloponnese; sometimes used to refer to all of Greece (and its people).

Achelous: an important river in western Greece.

Achilles: son of Peleus and Thetis; the greatest warrior of the Greeks at Troy.

Actaeon: Theban hero, son of Aristaeus and Autonoë; he offended Artemis and was torn apart by his own hunting dogs on Mount Cithaeron.

Adrasteia: goddess of necessity who punishes human arrogance.

Aeacus: legendary king of Aegina; father of Peleus and grandfather of Achilles.

Aegean: the sea to the east and south of mainland Greece.

Aegina: an island near Athens; in mythology, mother of Aeacus.

Aeneas: a Trojan chieftain; an important warrior against the Greeks.

Aenianian: referring to Aeniania, a small region in the south of Thessaly in north-central Greece.

Agamemnon: son of Atreus; leader of the Greek army at Troy; brother of Menelaus; husband of Clytemnestra; father of Iphigenia, Orestes, and Electra; on his return from the Trojan War he was murdered by Clytemnestra and her lover Aegisthus and was subsequently avenged by Orestes.

Agave: daughter of Cadmus; wife of Echion; sister of Semele, Ino, and Autonoë; mother of Pentheus.

Agenor: according to Greek mythology, a Phoenician hero; father of Cadmus.

Ajax: the name of two important Greek heroes during the Trojan War: the son of Telamon (the "greater" Ajax) from Salamis; and the son of Oileus (the "lesser" Ajax) from Locris.

Alexander: another name for Paris.

Alpheus: a river in the Peloponnese in southern Greece; it flows along Olympia, the site of an important religious center and the Olympic Games.

Althaea: wife of Oeneus, king of Calydon, a city in Aetolia (a mountainous area of central Greece on the northern coast of the Gulf of Corinth); when Dionysus stayed with Althaea and Oeneus as their guest, he fell in love with Althaea; Oeneus withdrew for a while, and Dionysus rewarded him for his graciousness by giving him the grapevine.

Aphrodite: goddess of sexual desire.

Apidanus: a river in Thessaly in north-central Greece.

Apollo: son of Zeus and Leto; twin brother of Artemis; god of prophecy, healing, archery, and poetry; his prophetic seat was at Delphi.

Ares: god of war.

Arethusa: the name of various fountains in ancient Greece; one was near the town of Chalcis in Euboea.

Argive(s): referring to the inhabitants of Argos; in general, all the Greeks.

Argos: a city and region in the eastern Peloponnese in southern Greece, site of an important temple of Hera; not always distinguished clearly from Mycenae.

Aristaeus: husband of Autonoë; father of Actaeon.

Artemis: daughter of Zeus and Leto; twin sister of Apollo; goddess of the hunt, childbirth, and virginity, who protected wild animals and boys and girls before they reached adolescence; sometimes identified with the goddess of the moon.

Asia: the region on the eastern coast of the Aegean Sea corresponding to modern Turkey and often referred to as Asia Minor.

Asopus: a river in Boeotia that flows near Thebes; in mythology, father of Aegina, who was the great-grandmother of Achilles.

Athena: daughter of Zeus and Metis; goddess of wisdom, warfare, and weaving; patron goddess of Athens.

Atreidae: Agamemnon and Menelaus (sons of Atreus).

Atreus: father of Agamemnon and Menelaus.

Attic: referring to the region of Attica in the east-central part of Greece dominated by and belonging to Athens.

Aulis: a harbor in eastern Greece in Boeotia, opposite Chalcis, at which the Greek fleet assembled in preparation for sailing to Troy.

Autonoë: daughter of Cadmus; wife of Aristaeus; sister of Semele, Ino, and Agave; mother of Actaeon.

Axios: an important river in Macedonia and northern Greece, now called Vardar.

Bacchae, bacchant: worshippers of Dionysus; Bacchae are specifically female, bacchants can be male.

Bacchic: referring to Bacchus (another name for Dionysus).

Bacchius: a male human celebrant of Dionysus, or Bacchus (Dionysus) himself.

Bacchus: another name for Dionysus.

Bactrian: referring to Bactria, a region in the western part of the Persian Empire, now comprising parts of Afghanistan, Pakistan, Uzbekistan, and Tajikistan.

Boeotia: a region in south-central Greece to the northwest of Attica.

Bromius: another name for Dionysus.

Cadmus: father of Semele, Agave, Autonoë, and Ino; grandfather of Actaeon and Pentheus; originally a Phoenician prince, son of Agenor; mythical founder of the Greek city of Thebes.

Calchas: the most important seer of the Greek army during the Trojan War.

Calypso: in the *Odyssey*, a sea nymph with whom Odysseus stayed for several years on his way home from Troy.

Capaneus: one of the seven champions against Thebes; father of Sthenelus.

Cape Malea: the most southeasterly peninsula of the Peloponnese in southern Greece.

Cassandra: Trojan princess, prophetic daughter of Priam and Hecuba; she was brought home by Agamemnon as his concubine and was murdered by Clytemnestra there.

Centaurs: wild creatures, half man, half horse, who inhabited Mount Pelion in Thessaly in north-central Greece.

Cephallenians: inhabitants of Cephallenia (now called Cephalonia), an island near Ithaca in the Ionian Sea west of mainland Greece.

Chalcis: the most important town on the island of Euboea, located on its west coast at the narrowest point of the Euripus channel, facing Aulis on the mainland.

Chiron: the gentlest and wisest of the Centaurs, who taught various heroes when they were children, including Achilles.

Cilicians: inhabitants of Cilicia, a kingdom on the southeastern coast of Anatolia (present-day Turkey).

Cithaeron: a mountain in central Greece near Thebes.

Clytemnestra: wife of Agamemnon; together with her lover Aegisthus she killed him on his return from Troy; mother of Iphigenia, Electra, and Orestes, who killed her in revenge for his father's death. Also written Clytaemestra.

Coroebus: son of Mygdon of Phrygia, an ally of the Trojans.

Corybantes: worshippers of the Phrygian goddess Cybele who danced to the sound of drums and pipes, bearing weapons and wearing crested helmets.

Corycia: a nymph who dwelled on Parnassus, associated with a cave (the Corycian Cave) on that mountain and the spring that flowed from there.

Crete: an important Greek island in the southeastern Mediterranean.

Cronian: referring to the primeval god Cronus, father of Zeus and many other Greek gods.

Curetes: worshippers of the Cretan goddess Rhea who danced to the sound of drums.

Cybele: a Phrygian goddess identified with Earth or Great Mother or Rhea.

Cyclops (plural Cyclopes): in the *Odyssey* and in Euripides' *Cyclops*, the Cyclops is a one-eyed primitive man-eating monster (named Polyphemus) whom Odysseus encounters on his way home from Troy; his neighbors (plural) are the Cyclopes. Elsewhere they are divine craftsmen who were supposed to have built the massive "Cyclopean" walls of Mycenae, Tiryns, Argos, and other cities.

Cypris, Cyprian: Aphrodite, who supposedly was born in the Mediterranean Sea near Cyprus and came first to land on that island; she was worshipped in an especially strong cult there.

Cyprus: an important Greek island in the southeastern Mediterranean.

Danaan, Danaans: descendants of Danaus; in general, Argives and, more generally, all the Greeks.

Danaus: a hero who was one of the legendary founders and kings of Argos.

Dardanus: a hero who was one of the legendary founders of Troy.

Delos: a Greek island in the Aegean Sea; birthplace of Apollo and Artemis and a center of their worship.

Delphi: the major oracle and cult center of Apollo, situated on Mount Parnassus in central Greece.

Demeter: goddess of cereal crops and fertility in general; mother of Kore/Persephone (queen of the underworld).

Diomedes: son of Tydeus; important Greek hero during the Trojan War; in the *Iliad*, together with Odysseus he spies on the Trojans and captures and kills Dolon.

Dionysus: son of Zeus and Semele; god of wine, music, and theater; also known as Bacchius, Bacchus, Bromius, Dithyrambus, Euhius, and Iacchus.

Dioscuri: Castor and Polydeuces (Pollux), the twin brothers ("Gemini") of Helen and Clytemnestra; sons of Zeus and Leda; divinities who protected mariners in distress.

Dirce: a fountain and river in Thebes.

Dithyrambus: a kind of choral poem in honor of Dionysus; also another name for the god Dionysus, sometimes explained in antiquity as referring to Dionysus' having been born twice, once from Semele and again from Zeus.

Dolon: a Trojan soldier; in the *Iliad* and *Rhesus* he spies on the Greeks and is captured and killed by Odysseus and Diomedes. His name in Greek suggests stealth or craftiness.

Eagle: a constellation of stars a couple of degrees north of the celestial equator.

Echinae: a group of islands in the Ionian Sea to the west of mainland Greece.

Echion: one of the surviving Sown Men who sprang up from the dragon's teeth sown by Cadmus; husband of Agave and father of Pentheus. His name in Greek suggests "viper."

Electra: daughter of Clytemnestra and Agamemnon; sister of Iphigenia and Orestes.

Electran gates: a city gate on the south side of Thebes toward Cithaeron.

Elis: a region on the northwest coast of the Peloponnese in southern Greece.

Enceladus: one of the Giants defeated by the Olympian gods; he was wounded by Athena.

Epeians: a people who lived in Elis on the northwest coast of the Peloponnese in southern Greece.

Eros: god of sexual desire, associated with Aphrodite.

Erythrae: a village in the northern foothills of Cithaeron going down toward the Asopus valley and Thebes.

Etna: a volcanic mountain in the eastern part of Sicily.

Euboea: island off the eastern coast of mainland Greece, north of Athens.

Euhius, Euhoian: referring to Dionysus; the epithets are derived from the ritual cry "Euhoi."

Euhoi: a ritual cry in honor of Dionysus.

Eumelus: a Greek warrior in the Trojan War; one of the suitors of Helen and one of the Greek soldiers who concealed themselves in the Trojan Horse; he participates as charioteer in the funeral games of Patroclus in book 23 of the *Iliad*.

Euripus: the narrow channel of water between the island of Euboea and the Greek mainland at Aulis.

Europa: a Phoenician princess who bore Sarpedon (a Lycian ally of the Trojans) to Zeus.

Eurotas: a river near Sparta in the Peloponnese in southern Greece.

Eurytus: the Greek commander of the Epeians from Elis and of the Taphians during the Trojan War.

Ganymede: a beautiful Trojan prince, abducted by Zeus to serve as his cup-bearer on Olympus.

Geraestus: site of a temple of Poseidon in the southern part of the island of Euboea.

Gerenian: from the town of Gerenia; a stock epithet for Nestor, king of Pylos.

Giant: one of the children of Earth, sometimes identified with the Titans, who fought against the Olympian gods and were defeated by them.

Gorgon: one of three monstrous snake-women who included Medusa, who was killed by Perseus; their faces were so terrifying that whoever looked on them was turned to stone.

Gouneus: the Greek commander of the Aenianians and Perrhaebians during the Trojan War.

Graces: companions of Aphrodite; goddesses of all kinds of beauty.

Hades: brother of Zeus and Poseidon; god of the underworld; his name is used synonymously for the underworld itself.

Harmonia: daughter of Ares; wife of Cadmus; mother of Agave, Autonoë, Ino, and Semele.

Hector: son of Priam and Hecuba; brother of Alexander/Paris; the greatest warrior of the Trojans against the Greeks; killed by Achilles.

Helen: daughter of Tyndareus; sister of Clytemnestra; wife of Menelaus (the brother of Agamemnon) and mother of Hermione; her (actual or putative) elopement with Paris caused the Trojan War.

Hellas: Greece.

Hephaestus: the divine blacksmith and craftsman of the Olympian gods; he was said to have his forges under the volcanic Mount Etna. Sometimes he is identified with the fire he used.

Hera: wife and sister of Zeus; queen of the gods; goddess of marriage; she had an important cult center at Argos.

Hermes: son of Zeus and Maia; the messenger god; god of travelers, contests, stealth, and heralds, who accompanied the souls of the dead to the underworld.

Hostile Sea: the Black Sea, traditionally difficult for sailors and inhabited by hostile peoples (the usual Greek name means "the hospitable sea" and was probably euphemistic).

Hysiae: a village in the northern foothills of Cithaeron going down toward the Asopus valley and Thebes.

Iacchus: another name for Dionysus.

Ida: a mountain near Troy, where Paris judged a beauty contest between Hera, Athena, and Aphrodite; Paris assigned the victory to Aphrodite, who rewarded him with Helen.

Ilium: Troy.

Inachus: the main river of Argos.

Ino: daughter of Cadmus; sister of Agave, Autonoë, and Semele.

Iphigenia: daughter of Agamemnon and Clytemnestra; when adverse winds blocked the Greek fleet at Aulis from sailing to Troy, Agamemnon had her brought to Aulis and was thought to have sacrificed her to Artemis there (though in some versions of the story Artemis spirited her away and put a deer in her place).

Ismenus: a river in Boeotia that flows through Thebes.

Ithaca: a Greek island in the Ionian Sea; home of Odysseus.

Laertes: father of Odysseus.

Land of the Blessed: a legendary, utopian land where a few heroes enjoyed a blissful life after death.

Leda: mythical queen of Sparta; wife of Tyndareus; she was visited by Zeus in the form of a swan; mother of Castor and Polydeuces, and of Helen and Clytemnestra.

Leitus: a Greek warrior from Boeotia during the Trojan War.

Leucadian rock: a cliff on the island of Leucas (now called Lefkada) in the Ionian Sea to the west of mainland Greece; plunging from it into the sea was connected with extreme sexual passion and other kinds of loss of self-control.

Libyan: referring to Libya, a region on the southern coast of the Mediterranean.

Locrian: referring to Locris, a region on the east-central coast of Greece, near Delphi.

Lycian: referring to Lycia, a region in southwestern Anatolia (present-day Turkey).

Lydia, Lydian: a region in west-central Anatolia (modern Turkey) and its inhabitants; its main city was Sardis.

Lydias: a river in Macedonia (modern Mavroneri).

maenad: ecstatic female worshipper of Dionysus.

Maia: a nymph, who bore Hermes to Zeus.

Maron: a priest of Apollo in Ismarus (a part of Thrace famous for its wine), who in the *Odyssey* gives Odysseus the wine he uses to get Polyphemus drunk.

Mecisteus: a legendary Greek warrior, son of Talus; father of Euryalus, who was famous for his skill as a boxer during the time of the Trojan War.

Media: a region of west-central Asia, and the ancient Iranian/Persian empire located there.

Meges: a Greek commander of the Epeians and Dulichians during the Trojan War.

Menelaus: brother of Agamemnon; husband of Helen.

Meriones: a Greek warrior during the Trojan War.

Musaeus: legendary poet and singer, sometimes associated with Athens and the Mysteries celebrated at nearby Eleusis.

Muses: daughters of Mnemosyne and Zeus, associated with all forms of cultural, especially artistic, musical, and poetic, excellence; one of the Muses bore Rhesus to Strymon.

Mycenae: an ancient city in Greece in the northeastern Peloponnese, not always distinguished clearly from nearby Argos.

Mygdon: king of Phrygia; father of Coroebus; an ally of the Trojans.

Myrmidons: a race of Greek warriors from Thessaly commanded by Achilles.

Mysian: inhabitant of Mysia, a kingdom in the northwestern part of Anatolia (present-day Turkey), near Troy.

Nereid: one of the fifty daughters of Nereus.

Nereus: a sea god; father of the fifty Nereids; famous for his wisdom.

Nestor: aged warrior and counselor of the Greek army during the Trojan War; king of Pylos; called Gerenian.

Nine, the: the Muses.

Nireus: one of the Greek warriors during the Trojan War, the handsomest after Achilles.

Nysa: an imaginary mountain associated with Dionysus and located in various parts of the world.

Odysseus: Greek warrior at Troy and hero of the *Odyssey*, which recounted his voyages back home to Ithaca after the Trojan War; son of Sisyphus or Laertes; famous for his cleverness.

Oeneus: legendary Greek king; father of Tydeus; grandfather of Diomedes.

Oenone: another name for the island of Aegina.

Oileus: father of one of the two Greek warriors at Troy named Ajax.

Olympus: a mountain on which the gods make their home, located in Pieria in northern Greece; also the name of a legendary Phrygian musician who was said to have invented the aulos (double pipe).

Orestes: son of Agamemnon and Clytemnestra; brother of Iphigenia and Electra; he killed his mother to avenge his father.

Orion: a legendary monstrous hunter, placed after his death among the stars as a constellation.

Orpheus: a mythical singer and lyre player associated with Thrace, able to attract animals and even stones by his song.

Orphic: referring to Orpheus, and the magic spells and salvation rituals associated with him.

paean: a kind of poem usually addressed to Artemis' brother Apollo and imploring or celebrating his help.

Paeonia, Paeonians: a region (and its inhabitants) in or near Thrace to the north of Greece in what is now Bulgaria and Macedonia.

Palamedes: Greek warrior at Troy; son of Nauplius, a descendant of Poseidon; he was treacherously killed by the Greeks through the machinations of Odysseus.

Pallas: Athena.

Pan: a rustic, musical god dwelling in wild nature and associated with sudden mental disturbances (hence our term "panic").

Pangaeum: a mountain in northeastern Greece.

Panthoüs: Trojan noble; father of Euphorbus, Hyperenor, and Polydamas.

Paphos: a city on the southwestern coast of Cyprus, near where Aphrodite was said to have been born and the site of an important temple in her honor.

Paris: also known as Alexander; son of Priam and Hecuba; his elopement with Helen caused the Trojan War.

Pelasgia: a vague geographical term that may refer to Arcadia, the Peloponnese, or all of Greece.

Peleus: husband of Thetis; father of Achilles.

Pelion: a mountain in the southeastern part of Thessaly in north-central Greece.

Pelops: son of Tantalus; mythical king of Pisa in the Peloponnese in southern Greece; origin of the Pelopids or Pelopidae, the royal dynasty of Argos which includes Atreus, Agamemnon, and Menelaus.

Pentheus: Theban king; son of Agave and Echion; grandson of Cadmus; cousin of Dionysus. His name in Greek suggests grief.

Pergamum: Troy.

Perseus: the legendary founder of Mycenae.

Pharsalia: a region in southern Thessaly in north-central Greece.

Pheres: father of Admetus, who was the father of Eumelus.

Philammon: father of Thamyris.

Phocis: a region in central Greece on the northern shore of the Gulf of Corinth.

Phoebe: according to Iphigenia in Aulis, a daughter of Leda; sister of Clytemnestra and Helen; otherwise little or nothing is known about her.

Phoebus: epithet of Apollo meaning "bright."

Phrygia, Phrygian, Phrygians: a kingdom (and its people) in west-central Anatolia (present-day Turkey); also often used as a synonym for Troy (and its people) or Trojan.

Phthia, Phthian: a region (and its people) in southern Thessaly in north-central Greece.

Phyleus: father of Meges.

Pieria: a mountainous region in the northern part of Greece; home of the Muses.

Pleiades: nymphs, daughters of Atlas, who were turned into a cluster of stars.

Polyphemus: in the *Odyssey* and Euripides' *Cyclops*, a man-eating primitive Cyclops whom Odysseus encounters on his way home from Troy; son of Poseidon.

Poseidon: brother of Zeus; god of the sea, of horses, and of earthquakes.

Priam: king of Troy; husband of Hecuba; father of Paris, Hector, and many other sons and daughters.

Protesilaus: Greek warrior, the first to die at Troy.

Pylos: an ancient town on the southwestern coast of the Peloponnese in southern Greece; home of Nestor.

Rhadamanthus: one of the judges of the dead in the underworld, famous for his justice.

Rhea: a Cretan goddess identified with Cybele; the Earth or Great Mother of the gods.

Rhesus: son of Strymon and a Muse; king of Thrace; ally of the Trojans; owner of extraordinary horses; killed by Odysseus and Diomedes. According to some versions, he would have been invincible if upon his arrival at Troy he and his horses had drunk from the Scamander River, but he was killed first.

Salamis: an island near Athens; home of the "greater" Ajax.

Sardis: an ancient city, capital of the ancient kingdom of Lydia, in western Anatolia (present-day Turkey).

satyrs: half-human, half-horse followers of Dionysus; said to be the sons of either Pan or Silenus.

Scamander: a river near Troy.

Scythian: referring to Scythia, a region to the northeast of Greece, around the Black and Caspian Seas; considered especially barbaric and savage.

Semele: Theban princess, daughter of Cadmus; mother of Dionysus by Zeus.

Sicilian sea: the sea to the east of Sicily, next to the Ionian Sea to the east.

Sicily: an island immediately to the southwest of Italy.

Sidon: one of the most important Phoenician cities, on the eastern coast of the Mediterranean (present-day Lebanon); the original home of Cadmus.

Silenus: an old, scurrilous companion of Dionysus and leader, or father, of the satyrs.

Simois: a river near Troy.

Sipylus: a mountain in Anatolia; home of Tantalus, the founder of the
   dynasty of the Pelopidae to which Agamemnon and Menelaus belonged.
Sisyphus: legendary founder of Corinth; in some versions the father of
   Odysseus; a trickster figure who famously deceived the gods on many
   occasions and was punished by having to roll a stone up a hill in the
   underworld that always rolled back when it neared the summit.
Sparta: an important city in the Peloponnese in southern Greece.
Sthenelus: son of Capaneus and Evadne; a Greek warrior associated with
   Diomedes during the Trojan War.
Strymon: father of King Rhesus of Thrace; also an important river in what
   is now Bulgaria and northern Greece.
Sunium: a cape at the southernmost point of the peninsula of Attica in
   southeastern Greece, site of a famous temple of Poseidon.
Taenarus: a cape at the southernmost tip of the Peloponnese in southern
   Greece, where there was said to be an entrance to the underworld.
Talaus: Greek hero; king of Argos and one of the Argonauts.
Talthybius: a herald of the Greek army at Troy, representing Agamemnon
   and the other leaders.
Tantalus: at *Iphigenia in Aulis* 505, a famous trickster, the son of Zeus, a fore-
   father of Agamemnon; at *Iphigenia in Aulis* 1150, another, much less cele-
   brated legendary figure, king of Pisa, first husband of Clytemnestra;
   killed by Agamemnon.
Taphian: referring to Taphos, an island in the Ionian Sea to the west of
   mainland Greece.
Teiresias: blind seer of Thebes; closely associated with Apollo.
Telamon: Greek hero from Salamis; father of the "greater" Ajax and Teucer.
Thamyris: son of Philammon; a mythical Thracian singer who challenged
   the Muses and was blinded by them for his presumption.
Thebes: a large city in Boeotia in central Greece.
Theseus: the most important hero of Athenian legend; father of Demophon
   and Acamas.
Thessaly, Thessalian: a large region (and its inhabitants) in the north-
   central part of Greece.
Thestius: father of Leda; grandfather of Phoebe, Clytemnestra, and Helen.
Thetis: sea nymph, one of the fifty daughters of Nereus; wife of Peleus and
   mother of Achilles.
Thrace, Thracians: a wild and primitive region (and its inhabitants) to the
   north of Greece in what is now Bulgaria and European Turkey, associ-
   ated with Dionysus and wine.
Thracian Sea: the northernmost part of the Aegean Sea, facing Macedonia,
   Thrace, and northwestern Asia Minor.

Thronium: a city in Epirus in the western part of mainland Greece.

Thymbraeum: an important temple of Apollo located near Troy.

thyrsus: a wand carried by worshippers of Dionysus, made of a fennel stalk with ivy vines and leaves wound around its tip and topped by a pine cone.

Tmolus: a mountain in Lydia in what is now western Turkey; Sardis lies at its base.

Triton: a divinity of the sea.

Troy, Trojans: a city (and its inhabitants) in northwestern Anatolia (present-day Turkey), defeated and pillaged by a Greek army after a long siege; also known as Ilium.

Troyland: another term for Troy and the surrounding region.

Tydeus: father of Diomedes.

Tyndareus: husband of Leda; putative father of Castor and Polydeuces, and of Helen and Clytemnestra.

Tyrrhenian: Etruscan; the people who lived along the coast of the Tyrrhenian Sea were notorious pirates. The war trumpet was thought to have been an Etruscan invention.

Zeus: king of gods and men.